WHEN DAWN BREAKS THE NIGHT

Melissa Aytche

ISBN 978-1-64003-338-2 (Paperback)
ISBN 978-1-64003-339-9 (Digital)

Copyright © 2017 Melissa Aytche
All rights reserved
First Edition

All rights reserved. No part of this publication may be reproduced, distributed, or transmitted in any form or by any means, including photocopying, recording, or other electronic or mechanical methods without the prior written permission of the publisher. For permission requests, solicit the publisher via the address below.

Covenant Books, Inc.
11661 Hwy 707
Murrells Inlet, SC 29576
www.covenantbooks.com

Prologue

In Revelations 12:11, you read: "And they have conquered him by the blood of the Lamb and by the word of their testimony, for they loved not their lives even unto death."

Most of us know him as Tony, short for Anthony, but only his immediate family can get away with that part. Tony is what he prefers to be called today as part of the man he has become. His past often haunts him. When storms come, there is always a piece of Tony that is waiting for the other shoe to drop. He has seen a darkness that most could not imagine.

Tony may seem like just another person from the projects that grew up poor and in an environment that can so easily suck you in and drag you under, but his history is who he was and not who he is today.

Through many bad choices, he created a life full of destruction, but God had a different plan for him and through his darkest days, God was present. Still not flawless, still not without sin, but there is a light with Tony that exists in his way with people, the way his heart goes to those that are suffering, and how he sees those that are often ignored.

We all have a past. Your past may or may not be the same, but that is okay. There is a freedom you experience when you share your life and there is a weight that is lifted when you use it to help others. We are asked in the Bible to not keep our past a secret but to use it for the glory of God. This can seem painful, but imagine how wonderful it would feel if you were able to help someone else from suffering your same fate.

The words of your testimony are powerful words. They are the pieces that shaped you, but also the ability to walk with others in like situations. God can heal you from the pain. It may always be a part of who you are, but it does not need to define who you will become. Each of us has a purpose regardless of our struggles.

What keeps most people from sharing their story is shame. Even if the events were not of your own doing, we carry shame. That is what has kept this story from being told for so long. One thing I have learned over the years is shame is an emotion that is meant to keep us living in the pain.

In the book of Genesis, you read about Joseph's life and how it is like many of ours. He was betrayed by his brothers and made a slave, falsely accused by a woman, and put in jail only later to become a prominent leader. Do you think this came without emotion? Of course not, but it was his faith in God that carried him through and assured him that despite his hardest times, he was special in the eyes of God, and he was destined for more than the pain he had in those years.

Some stories are harder to tell than others, but it does not lessen the shame you feel. Sometimes the stories that can change lives are the ones that are the hardest to tell. Maybe that is why we felt so compelled to write this story. Shame is a lie whispered into your ear to keep you from speaking your truth.

The reality is we are not free from sin. It is the war that we go through in this life as the battle of good and evil. We all fall short at times, and what we need is not someone who will judge us but walk with us. I know that when I feel hurt and pain, I seek out the ones I know I can trust to help guide me through it. I especially call on those that can say "Me too, but here is how God saved me."

Over the years as Tony reflected on his past, it occurred to him that there were people in his life that were a light in his darkness, and those people didn't even know that this is what they were doing. They did not boast about being a light. They just loved on him when he was unlovable and through their actions his light was able to overcome his darkness.

When you see others that are down, do you judge them? Do you look for how you are better? Do you reach back and put out a hand and walk with them? I have heard the lines, "Be kind as you do not know what others are walking through." This is by far one of the biggest truths I have learned in my relationship with Tony. God gave you grace. Why should someone else not get the same?

Tony fully intended to live his life and this part of it locked away. For years we have talked about telling others, and he would always say, "Someday, maybe," but there comes a point where the pieces you lock away are needed in the lives of others. I am sure he always knew it was coming, but hoped the day would not come.

When I felt the calling to help Tony write this story, I knew it would not be an easy task. I knew when approached about finally telling his story, he would not come easily. I broached the subject lightly and told him my vision. I let Tony sit in that for a few days and then approached him again. Each time his eyes would change, and you could see the pain return. He never said no, but you could tell it was not an easy thing I was asking him to do.

Now, some might ask why a book? The truth is this is Tony's life, but it is God's story. It is not about him as much as it is about the miracles that God performs in our lives. It is when you know you should not be alive and yet here you stand facing the world today. This is why a book, because there is something in knowing that God saved him just like God can save you.

Tony's life is a miracle, and his name may not be known by the world, yet his life has impact—his life filled with poverty, drugs, alcohol, anger, abandonment, and more. Yet, through it all, you cannot help but see God working in him.

Recently listening to sermons online from various influences, the common theme is repeated about how God does not waste pain. I believe it is Pastor John Gray that not only says this often but has also said you are not sentenced to pain but entrusted with it. Tony's story has been entrusted to him, but he has been living the sentence of this pain for over thirty years.

After careful consideration and a whole lot of prayer, Tony said yes. Maybe it is time for you to say yes? Maybe it is time for healing? Maybe, just maybe you are very close to this story in your own life, and you can see God's hands faster than he did. Our prayer and belief is this is a story that people need to hear. God's grace and love saved him from a lifetime of pain, and he can do it for you.

As I sit here next to Tony as he is ready to share his life to you, I cannot help but notice just how full of love for life he is and just how much he loves his family. His life today is filled with joy which has made him tentative to go back into this part of his life.

The Decision

As Tony begins to tell me his events, you can see his face transform to another time, and you cannot help but feel like the person talking is not the same person who lived these events all those years ago. Yet the look in his eyes as he recalls the pieces will tell you otherwise.

During this process, Tony often will need to get up and take a break or do something to keep moving. It is his way of trying hard to escape some of the memories and the stirring of emotion in him. Tony is a strong man and being vulnerable is not something he is used to.

Many do not know this man, but I do. Tony is my husband, and I know how hard it is to press into this part of his life. What a strong person it takes to keep coming back and fighting through the emotion and plugging through to get this out.

Like many people that finally get away from their situations that kept them down, they bury it deep within and would much rather forget about it, but somehow it always seems to come back up. Tony has quite literally moved thousands of miles away from the city he called home, and yet the streets still call his name.

The further away Tony went, the easier it was to not share this part of his life, and he had always thought that when God set him free, he was fully healed. It wasn't until it was time to tell this story in detail that the pain returned in great force. God has asked him to face this past for his healing.

In May, Tony turned fifty years old. This is something I know he is not thrilled for others to hear, but it is significant as it has meant a milestone that he only dreamed would happen when he was a little boy. For days before his birthday, he sat in some reflection about where he was in life.

There was a time in his life where this was not even a blip on his radar. Tony had not yet reached all of his dreams, but the life he has was a far cry from the life he came from. So, in his reflection, Tony was torn by the memories of his past and the reality that he was still here.

Ultimately he understood just how very blessed he was to be where he was at. He is married with a stepdaughter and a son. He lives in a nice house in Southern Arizona. He drives a nice car, and he helps put food on the table and keeps a roof over our heads. This on top of being able to give back will make for huge accomplishments in his life that he did not expect after growing up in the projects. He is humbled by just how much he was able to achieve when he let God into his life.

It often amazes Tony how so many people take this all for granted. How sometimes he even will take his life now for granted. How easy it is to get in those routines. How easy it is to get frustrated that things are not moving fast enough.

Tony still talks about something he heard from Joyce Meyer during one of her sermons, "If you are always in a hurry, then a relationship with God can be frustrating." God's timing is not our timing and usually if you have to wait a bit, you find that there is so much more available to you, but being slightly impatient, the waiting can be the hardest part.

Tony is hit with the humbleness that he should not have even been here in these routines or contemplating his growth and anxiously awaiting on the next phase of his life. As a man, he can quickly forget how fast it can all be gone, yet the younger version of him is always a reminder that he cannot live like there is no other way.

As a father, he believes in humbleness, respect, and spoiling. He can seem strict at times, but Tony wants them to have everything he did not and to teach them everything he wished he knew when he was their age. He had grown up not knowing much about what a father should do and takes pride in those lessons every day.

As he sat there before his birthday, he was filled with peace. God had given Tony this life, and now after all these years, it was time to share the whole story. As Tony went out to the pool to do a few laps, he spent some time in his thoughts, and his path became clear. It was time for his fear of judgment to face the God he knows.

If you start to feel like it is too late for God to save you, then you need this story. The devil's work is to convince you that you are just not good enough to be saved, but that is not the heart of God. It was God who saved Tony when he was unlovable to the world, and Tony knows firsthand that it is never too late.

> The Good man brings good stored up in his heart. The evil man brings evil stored in his heart, for out of the overflow of his heart his mouth speaks. (Luke 6:45).

Tony knows the evil that can come forth from his mouth and his actions when you are experiencing extreme situations. It broke down his ability to hold productive relationships and was fueled by anger. Only God can break down the walls in your heart if you let him. This is something Tony has learned over the years, and today his life reflects the good built up in his heart.

Search your heart and ask God where you need to heal? Where do you need to set aside shame and share your story?

Our Family Life

> But if serving the lord seems undesirable to you, then choose for yourselves this day whom you will serve, whether the gods your ancestors served beyond the Euphrates, or the gods of the Amorites, in whose land you are living. But as for me and my household, we will serve the lord.
>
> —Joshua 24:15, NIV

Every morning for many years, Tony has held a consistent routine. As he arises for work extra early so he can get it all completed in time, he likes the time to get a small workout in, get a protein shake, time to read the Bible, and shower before leaving. It is Tony's time to be with God as he prepares for the day ahead.

At night, the two of us will lie in bed several hours before going to sleep. A routine established many years ago. This is our sanctuary and a place we can talk and not be disturbed. It may seem strange, but this is where we have peace, and we can lie down the stress of the day and just enjoy each other's company.

I would tell you that some of our best ideas, reconciliations, and discussions have happened in this sanctuary. This is where you can see Tony at his most vulnerable away from what the outside world gets to view.

Meeting Tony, you immediately notice how much he loves to joke and loves to laugh. I am sure there are people who probably think he never takes anything serious, but his smile is contagious, and he is enjoying life. I believe he just loves laughing at his own jokes, but laughter is a key for him after all these years. He has an often sarcastic humor or suggestive humor, and we have a lot of fun taking shots at each other.

On the flipside of his laughter, Tony is a very honest person and is not afraid to say what he thinks. As I am more of a nurturer, this can be difficult at times, but there is nothing fake about his interactions. He will always tell you like it is and expects nothing less in return.

We met in an unlikely place where I was out to dance, and he was out spending time with a few friends. So it was in a dance club that we met for the first time. Now I have heard about how many relationships don't last when you meet in these environments, but this was not an "I was watching you from across the room" story.

I was not in the mood to talk with anyone as I was upset that my friend had disappeared once again leaving me standing there alone. So when Tony came in irritated with his friends and what they were doing, he came and stood by me.

Both of us irritable and ready to go home standing in this club, we ended up right next to each other. As he noticed me, he knew I was not happy and just simply asked, "Why are you so angry?" It is funny when you think about it because we have not looked back since. We had an instant connection and quite literally spent the rest of the night talking, laughing, and dancing.

I was a single mom when I met Tony, and he has been the father figure in my daughter's life. Knowing that she did not have much of a relationship with her father, he just picked it up. Not knowing how to be a father himself, he will admit to many mistakes, but loving her was never one of them.

He has always been adamant that her father should be in her life. Stemming from the absence of a father in Tony's life, he never wanted to take the place of the future with her father. Seeing the reality of the situations, he wanted to give her what he did not have, so in the absence of her father, he raised her.

Tony was beaming with pride when she graduated high school, and he is looking forward to her next graduation from college this year. Like most father-daughter relationships, he has met only one person that he feels would be good enough for her. He finds joy in seeing her happy and knows how beautiful and smart she is.

Now a grown woman, Tony tells anyone who will listen about the beautiful smart woman she has become. As we prepared to move last year to Arizona, the hardest part for both of us had to let her go so she can start her life. She will always be the "Little Girl" to him.

When you come from the streets of New York, you often get nicknames. Many of them do not make sense outside of that world, but it is a sign of love and respect. Right or wrong, she got the name *Little Girl*, and it stuck. She may not be little anymore, but she will always have that piece in Tony's heart.

It is almost daily that you will find Tony with some kind of noise in the background. He loves listening to music, and it will often get on my nerves as he consistently turns on seventies' music and has it blasting through the house. Now, there is nothing against the oldies of the seventies, and I do like some of the songs, but me, I like more variety.

It is when that music goes on that means things are about to get done. For those that know Tony, that would mean quite frequently. Even if you wanted to sit and relax, the music is his queue for time to work. This is when he goes into his cleaning modes, and often side by side we usually get the house fully cleaned.

Tony is a little on the OCD side when it comes to cleanliness. This is something he carried over from his past. It can be quite maddening at times, but is probably one of the things I love most about him. Well, other than he does all the laundry in the house and I don't have to.

I am sure a lot of gentlemen are not happy with me I just said that. Tony did not like the way I sorted laundry and said he would handle it. That was it, and he has done it ever since. The good part for me is he actually enjoys it and has only turned my whites pink one time.

We each have our thing that we just handle, and the things we share in. Tony's is the laundry, and mine is anything that involves a computer while we share in the cooking and the cleaning. It works for us, and we make a great team. Sorry, gentlemen, if I ruined it for you, but this is something as a woman I do not miss.

Tony will tell you he loves to cook, but don't be fooled by the cooking part. When you meet Tony, he will tell you he is a chef, but in reality, he has a menu he can cook that usually involves chicken and rice. This man can eat rice every single day and be content. Again, there is nothing against eating rice, but I like variety. I am pretty sure to this day our daughter does not eat rice, and if she does, it is sparingly.

If you want a taste of some amazing things, Tony can make some mean fried chicken, fried pork chops, or fried catfish. These are foods that speak to his soul, and you can taste the love when he is done. These are reminders of his mom, and he takes great care in making it the way she used to. As you get older, fried foods are not as common. He does not make these often and usually requires one of us begging him to do it, but man when he does, it is wonderful.

So with fried foods being a smaller part of our diet, he has now expanded his horizons with a smoker. Move over fried food, I think we may have created an animal on the smoker. Not a joke. Tony smokes some kind of meat every single weekend. I do not mind though as the joy on his face when it comes out perfect is joy in my heart as well. Who knows, maybe he will be on one of those grill master shows someday.

There is a gift Tony has been given in his life, and one that I like to call the gift of being a socialite. Extrovert would be an understatement to this man. He talks to everyone he encounters.

Tony does not like it when I tell him this, but he could sell ice to an Eskimo with his charm and style. I am sure that is his modest side, but when I ventured into the jewelry business, it was Tony who helped me get three-fourth of my customers.

No fear of anything and especially people has been enlightening over the years. It does not matter your race, sizes, gender, and walk of life, he will most likely befriend you if you let him. It is most often done with Tony breaking the ice with his laughter and a smile.

I have learned that you never know who you will meet when you give people half the chance. In his lifetime, Tony has met so many wonderful people. You have probably been to our home for one of our many parties over the years. He loves to entertain and spend time with people. The sheer variety and walks of life that we have had the privilege of spending time with is truly super natural.

As a couple, we are pretty competitive and love to play games. Something we both carry over from our childhood, and you might see us whip out a football, volleyball net, or basketball, and challenging you to a match. When my son turned twelve, Tony was out in the street with all the boys playing football. He was a kid again and got to enjoy just the time spent playing.

Our son loves football, and daddy loves to watch him play. I often tease Tony as he is "that" father. You know the father that walks up and down the sidelines with each play shouting instruction, giving encouragement, or just cheers of excitement. Now mind you, this does not make him the coach of the team, but that does not matter. I am not sure what he will do now that they actually have stands for the parents.

Tony has only missed one game his son has played because of work. The game was a playoff that had to be made up during the week because of weather. He worked his butt off to get there on time, and just as he was walking up, the last play of the game took place. My son's team lost that game, and by their reaction, you would think they both lost. It means so much to Tony to watch his son play, and missing those games is something he truly despises.

Our life has not been all peaches and sunshine. We have weathered our share of storms through our marriage. The many storms usually come in our family, storms in our relationship, and storms in our finances. These storms were meant to destroy our relationship, and as you can tell, our marriage has won so far.

There have been a few of those times that we probably could have given up very easily, and no one would have blamed us for splitting. Yet, God had a different plan, and each time we would come out stronger and wiser. We have learned that storms will come, but as promised, it will pass, and the other side of the storm is glorious.

Our marriage is not different than most, but marriage is hard work. It takes love, patience, a few times of walking away to calm down, laughter, and most importantly communication. We are stronger together, and after sixteen years, we know that with God and hard work, we will pull through.

Through Tony's life, he has learned the value of serving others. He will open his door and serve you a meal. He will offer you anything from drinks, to conversation, to laughter, and almost always food. It is Tony's servant heart that I most fell in love with.

Whenever Tony is out, you will see him stop and care for even those that have nothing. He often will not even wait for them to ask, but instead he will just offer. He has taken criticism for that, but unless you know his story, you may never understand. Tony does not like to boast about this to others as it is not about him. It is about his need to help others that are down.

As you walk into the door of our home, you can see just how important family is to him. The walls covered with family photos and memories of his life. Even if I wanted to do other decorating, there has to be space for memories on the wall. This is his daily reminder of how far Tony has come, how much work he has done at being a father, and how to live in joy.

Tony is a hard worker and for many years has not taken that for granted. Even when frustrated in the jobs he has had, he did not slack off. He would have to be extremely sick and unable to move for him not to show up for work. His desire to work hard for everything has been a blessing in our relationship and are the fruits of the seeds sown into him as a young child.

I believe it is Tony's ability to talk to people has helped break down barriers and build bridges. The bridges for us are so important because at first glance we look different. At times we have faced situations where when we are out together, we get a few stares, or have people move away from us. No, we do not stink, but there are just people who will not accept us as a couple because all they see is the color of our skin.

As baffling as that is to both of us and almost comical to the extent of which some people will go to avoid us, we both usually laugh. It is not worth allowing those few to rob us of our joy. Instead of getting angry, we usually just smile and go our own way. Not everyone will understand, but they do not have our heart or our story and that is okay. Tony still is going to talk to everyone, and he is still going to build bridges.

Joy comes for us in our ability to talk. We are best friends, and we talk about everything. Many times in reminiscing about the pure good times we have had, and how even in certain storms we found joy. People must think we are a little crazy on how much we talk to each other, but we would not have it any other way.

When I met him, he carried a strong faith in God. It took a while for us to find a church, and to be honest, a few times we pretty much gave up looking. Yet, through it all, God showed up through our little girl, and she guided us to a church we called home for years.

Tony often jokes now that we are in Arizona and once again on the search for a church that we need her come out here and guide us to the right church. She has never steered us wrong when it came to that. Thanks to a host of great friends and spiritual family, we stay grounded in our search today.

This is the joy in Tony's heart and one that overflows in how he talks to people today. Even if you are in a storm right now, what are some of the things you have that you can reflect on and have joy?

A Glimpse

> Be strong and courageous. Do not be afraid or terrified because of them, for the Lord your God goes with you; he will never leave you nor forsake you.
>
> —Deuteronomy 31:6

Patience is not Tony's strong suit and something he has to work at. I would say there are a lot of people just like him in this sense. After all, have you seen how people drive lately? It does not matter what city you are in, everyone is always in a hurry, and patience runs thin. His career has been driving trucks both over the road and local, so his impatience for drivers stems from years of experience.

I remember the first time he took me to his hometown in New York. It was right after 9/11, and tensions were still very high. My family was nervous that we were going, but Tony assured them all would be okay. This was the city where Tony had grown up, so he had a strong need to go back home.

This trip, he rented a car so he could show me the whole city. We had a room in Manhattan, and his family was in Brooklyn. Driving through the city, I do not think I looked out the front windshield unless we were stopped. The rest of the time my hand was on that oh crap bar, and I looked out the side window all while he got great joy in seeing me squirm. I just could not watch him or any other driver for that matter maneuver that city. Yet, we always ended up at our destination just fine.

Tony found it quite funny how I refused to look out the window as he drove. He even offered to let me drive in which I happily declined. So when he parked the car at the hotel and said we could take the subway, I was beyond thrilled.

My first trip to New York was an extremely unique experience. I was a tourist, but not in the way you would ever think. In all of our trips there, I have never been to Central Park or the Statue of Liberty. I did tell Tony that someday he would have to take me to do the true touristy thing in which he laughs but agrees.

My experience was one that gave me a glimpse into his world and with that comes a whole lot of perspective. He took me to his old home in the projects of Brooklyn. This is where he grew up most of his childhood, and his family was there gathering together.

The projects were unlike anything I had seen. When you arrive in the city, there is a distinct smell of exhaust and fuel, but in the projects, you often get the smell of hot pee in the doorways and elevators of the buildings.

I still remember Tony warning me about where I stood in the elevator and to do my best to not touch the sides. I was in a whole different world than where I had come from as I tried to soak it all in.

As we arrived at the apartment, he introduced me to many members of his family. Having almost his whole family together in the old apartment did not strike me as supernatural until later when I knew more of his story.

We ate, we talked, and we laughed during dinner with his family. I had my first taste of collard greens and admittedly they had to grow on me. Tony's father was there and would comment on how many times he got up for more food. He would just laugh, but he was eating his momma's food after many years away, and he was not going to waste any of it.

For the most part, his family was very welcoming to me. His father just grunted when I spoke, but everyone else seemed to be genuinely gracious. We had only been together for a short time before that trip, but Tony was happy to introduce me to his family.

I had known some of the stories from his childhood, but being there, you had a sense there was a lot more to tell. You definitely had the sense that the streets held a secret or two, but he had not known me long enough to share. Yet with a smile on his face, Tony took me throughout the whole city, and I was able to see and experience the environment in which he was raised.

We took the time to walk the entire perimeter of the 9/11 destruction site. It was still in the cleanup process, and the noise of the cranes and the smell of molding metal were distinct reminders.

There was a small walkway bridge you could walk out over the site and see it all. We did not choose to do this part, but it was important to walk the entire way around. We walked slowly, and it took us several hours stopping only to read stories and look at the pictures. It was a somber experience for both of us, but especially for him.

It was personal to Tony as this city was his home. He knew the struggles of the people there, and he felt helplessness. He could not do much at that point, so instead he prayed and made sure he took the time to pay tribute to all of the victims.

After walking around the site, we found a restaurant nestled a few stories up overlooking some of the damage. It was extremely humbling to sit there and look over, but you could almost reconstruct aspects as he would tell me stories about his experiences in the towers and shared the memories of his times there.

It had been a while since he had been home, and he was shocked at how much it had changed. One thing that had not changed much was just how many people he still knew there. It was not uncommon during that trip for a ten-minute walk from the apartment to the train to take over an hour. This was mostly because Tony could not walk down the street without running into someone from his past. Of course this is where you learn just how social he is with people and the joy he feels in his relationships.

Being with Tony, I was always safe. He was right there by my side, and it was clear that he had respect in the neighborhood, so I was left alone. Of course that did not happen without his stern warnings for me to not just go off on my own. I was out of place, and they knew it, but the respect for him kept me protected.

This is one of the first times I really understood how Tony protects the ones he cares about. It is almost a fierce protection, and something he does instinctively. I will not lie, it is almost annoying; all the locks, poles, alarms he will put on our home even today.

After we moved into our home in Arizona, he did not like how the doors locked, so he had to go get extra locks just to be sure. However, once I had seen his environment and understood his life, I could see why Tony is so protective of his family.

This trip for me was amazing and so much better than the touristy pieces. Seeing the city from the eyes of someone else is something you cannot describe. That trip drew us closer together and instinctively we knew we would be together after that. I had been given a glimpse into his world and did not run screaming. We have been back to the city a few times since with both kids, and their experience of New York is not much different.

There is one thing that Tony has come to fully understand and that is when it is time to leave. As much as he loves the people and his family, those streets are a pull that he cannot ignore. The trip may have held some nostalgia of his past, but there was a pain in those streets, and he could not stay.

Many times we are given a glimpse into the lives of people, but we do not always seem to know the whole story. I certainly knew I did not know the whole story, but the most important part for me was to get the view and not compare it to my own experience. When you get the glimpse of others even if brief, how do you react?

Points of View

> And be not conformed to this world: but be ye transformed by the renewing of your mind, that ye may prove what is that good, and acceptable, and perfect, will of God.
>
> —Romans 12:2

The man I know is a great man that is full of faults, full of love, and maybe a little quirky. Over the last twenty-five years, if you met Tony, I would say the man you met was the man he is today, but you have glimpsed pieces of who he used to be. Much of his past has shaped his points of view in life today.

He grew up poor and did not expect handouts from anyone. He is a firm believer even today about the power of working for what you have. This mentality has helped save him in many areas of his life. It is a mentality that he still carries today and works to pass on to the children.

So when he sees others that feel entitled to things, he is really bothered. Everything he was given as a child was for survival. He had the love of his mother, but there was discipline too. The environment he grew up in meant you were not picky about what you ate. You ate what was there, or you did not eat at all. You did not get to go and get the top fashion in clothes just because everyone else had it. You get what could be afforded if not handed down from siblings.

He loves his sneakers. He takes great care of them, and he has pairs that are over ten years old that practically look new. Why? Well, like the clothes, you did not get a choice of the latest style or brand. Oftentimes him and his brothers would get the cheapest sneaker around, and I am sure his mother was not always thrilled that they would wear through them in weeks.

We love to give our kids some nice things when we can, but never do they get things because they are entitled to it. In our house, our children do not demand anything and expect to get it. In fact, if they demanded anything, I am sure they will find out quickly as to what they can lose. Not that they haven't tried from time to time, but the experience quickly taught them to not press further.

I am sure some parents would agree, and I am sure some will not, but your kids are entrusted to you from God. You cannot choose to be their friend over their parent. That is not the purpose. Think about it; if you got everything you asked God for right when you asked for it, you would never be grateful for the things he does give you and how perfect his timing is when God gives them to you.

If our kids choose to not value what is given, then they are the ones that have to work to replace those things so they can understand the work we put in so they can have those items. Sowing into them the value of working hard and appreciating what is given is so very important to Tony. Being a straight talker, you can almost bet that if he feels that what we provide is being taken advantage of, you are most likely going to hear about it.

A stunned silence has been the reaction to the few that Tony has allowed into his past. Yet in all the darkness, the power of the love of God is so evident in him. It has taken years to understand that Gods pursuit of him was relentless. It took time so walls could be broken down, but when he was ready, he was able to receive the gift and appreciate it so much more. He was not entitled to the grace he was given, he was just given the grace out of love. This is something that cannot be replaced, and one you cherish throughout life.

"Greater is the one living inside of you, than he who is living in the world" (1 John 4:4).

As he reflects on what God has done for him, it has become important for him to understand that even the most broken, the most lost, the most hurt can be found by God. His relentless pursuit of us is one of the biggest displays of love we can ever receive.

Think back to when you were dating. There was an element of wanting to be pursued by the other as a sign of affection. Do you remember the letdown when you did not get it? Well, God always pursues us, and as the verse reflects, that is so much greater than anything man alone can provide.

Recently, a friend of Tony's had been sick. He talked with him on the phone since he was a few states away and tried to encourage him to seek the help he needed. He made several phone calls to other friends asking them to intervene personally. They all promised they would, but none found the time. A week later, that friend took his life.

Now, there was nothing anyone really could have done. You can always say what if they had intervened, but that is almost always a difficult part of suicide. Tony's friend was lost, and the pain was too much to handle. When people reached out, his friend would respond, but his heart was not hearing the whispers of life and hope. This is close to Tony and the events of his story. The parts where hope seems futile, and there is the feeling that the pain will never end.

Understanding the power the devil tries to have in our lives can be a bit baffling. It is whispers of destruction. It is the fuel of hate the devil seeks. God seeks you when you are alone, and you feel there is nothing left. It is often a common feeling of those that live in the projects that the ones that make it out are the lucky ones. What I find fascinating are those that make it out of the streets will wear the logo of the city they came from as a badge of honor, and one that says I survived.

Tony survived the streets by only the grace of God. He will tell you that over and over as he knew that he should have never made it out alive.

There are many statistics that follow an environment Tony came from. Some he quotes frequently as a reminder that many will end up stuck in poverty, they will be in jail, or they will be dead. Very few actually get out unscathed in some way, but once you get out, there is a freedom you could not imagine.

Sometimes the point of view is shaped by your experience. It has been important for Tony to teach the value that comes in respecting others and most certainly the gifts you're given. What are some of the values you hold dear to your heart? Do they line up with the word of God?

The Little Boy

> But we proved to be gentle among you, as a nursing mother tenderly cares for her own children.
>
> —1 Thessalonians 2:7

Tony was a young child that grew up in the projects of Brooklyn. He was the second to the youngest of nine children. There was an older brother he never met as he passed away as a young child, so he grew up in a house with three older brothers, three older sisters, and just him and his brother at the bottom.

Some of his earliest memories come when they were living in an old building that put him and two other brothers on the floor of the living room to sleep. With this small apartment, Tony often would describe it as living with rats the size of cats. Not having a bed to sleep on and the screaming that came when they had to jump from the floor to the couch when the rats would come in.

The memories of that building are sketchy at best since he was so very young. He does remember not living there long, and the building being condemned. This is when they moved to an apartment in the projects of Brooklyn.

To a small boy, the apartment was like a mansion. It was a five-bedroom apartment that was several floors up the stairway. They had a two-story apartment where the rooms were upstairs, and to him it was huge. This was so much more than the place they lived in before and would be the home Tony grew up in.

This also meant no longer sleeping on the floor of the living room. Tony had a bed and shared a room with his little brother. He may have been young, but the value of having a bed and only sharing with one brother was a huge improvement. There was enough space for them to stretch out, and each had their own little space.

The apartment was just a walking distance to shopping and the train. That would make it very convenient for those in the area to not have a car to get around. Tony's mom did have a station wagon for all the kids for when they would need to go further, but most of the time they did walk for what they needed.

Being so young, the view Tony first remembers is a far cry from reality. He was so little at the time and did not know what was in store. Each of the eight would have their lives built and shaped in this apartment they called home. It was a nice new beginning for him and his family.

Tony was five when his mom and dad divorced and his dad left. He was very young but remembers them arguing a lot and then one day his dad being gone. He and his little brother were too little to really understand the impact of this unlike his older siblings.

Over the years, the others tell him stories about that time, but to him he was just gone. He remembers that his father would come to see them from time to time but that would fade away. The father they needed really was not there.

His mom took a job and would work long hours on an overnight shift just to keep food on the table, the ability to pay the bills, and keep clothes on their backs. As Tony remembers his earliest childhood, it was always Mom, and she was always hard at work. She was a strong woman that never seemed to waiver in the hard times. Throughout his life, he would hold a special bond with his mother and even when times were tough, he would always want to help her.

Over the years, Tony would have little to no interaction with his father. Sadly, where he is from this is not uncommon. In the projects, many like him were raised by their mothers. Many of the fathers were in jail, gone, or dead leaving the influence of the streets as their teacher. Having both parents in the home was the exception and not the rule.

It was not until he was twenty years old that he would have some semblance of a relationship with his father. As he was younger, the absence of Tony's father put him in a search for others to fill this role. Only in the projects it would not be an easy thing to find.

His mom was his love. Oh how many times Tony would see her work to the bone to take care of the family. He recalls the many times his mom would come home after a night of work, make breakfast for the family, get the kids off to school, all before she could get rest. She took care of this family on her shoulders, and it did not go unnoticed.

Despite the difficulty of the situation, his mother always had food on the table; she always had clothes on their back and would even find time to pile all the kids into the car for a family road trip. These are the memories Tony cherishes to this day. He was always an explorer, and seeing the world outside of the city gave him a different lens to view from even if only for a while.

They would often travel to North Carolina and spend time with family there. It was a week they all looked forward to every year. It was their chance to get out and experience life outside of the city. Tony was still so young, but he remembers those trips like they were yesterday.

These were seeds his mom sowed into him. The seeds of working hard and the seeds of adventure were instilled into him and would be the things that played a big role in his life later on. Like his mom, he loved adventure and the world outside of the city block they lived on.

Later in life when Tony's mother had suffered another stroke, he would sit with her and talk. Oh the stories she could tell you about how she was raised, the pain she suffered, and her struggle. It wasn't all pain as she shared her passion for traveling, and there was no mistaking her love of the NY Mets.

In all the talks they had, one key thing kept coming up in those conversations. How there were so many times she was not sure how she would pay a bill or have money for food, and every single time

God provided. The smile on her face helps you to understand that even in hard times she was given joy.

Tony's mom was a woman of faith, and she would ensure that he and his family would go to church on Sundays. After church were some of his great memories. His mom would always take time to cook a big meal for the family.

He can still remember her making a spread fit for a king. Still seeing her carefully batter up the fried chicken and putting her collard greens on to simmer. She would always whip up a batch of her cornbread, and he can still smell the sweet potato pie cooking in the oven. It was food for the soul that was prominent in his home, and he loved his momma's cooking.

These were the days Tony loved. During the week, they would make do with the Corn Flakes, the bologna, or even grits. On Fridays they would have fish, but every Sunday afternoon they were able to sit down and have a feast.

This has been hard to live up to as I was not the greatest cook when we met. I was learning, but my style was vastly different. Many times he would say how much he missed his momma's cooking. I could have taken that personal, but she was a good cook. Thankfully though, she taught me a few things in the kitchen and Tony paid attention to how she cooked and he can handle the rest.

Tony loved being outdoors and would often go out to play. You would often find him on the handball courts, in the streets playing football or baseball. These are just some sports that would draw him in and fill his early childhood.

He especially loved handball, and like many of his friends, Tony was very good at playing. So often the tournaments they would hold would find him somewhere toward the top of the chain. He had a talent for sports, but living in the projects you did not play on grass or in any organized leagues. You played in the streets, and only the streets.

In the inner city, there was no funding for activities such as organized sports, the arts, music, or more. This statistic has unfortunately not changed much in his old neighborhood. Many kids grow up in the inner city only able to play in the streets or move elsewhere to get these advantages. The money for these programs is scarce and is sadly spreading throughout the country today.

Imagine how many lives would be different if there were those activities available that would help keep so many of them off the streets? It helps keep them focused on more than their situations, it helps them grow and enjoy life. In the inner city, you were on the streets to play, but that is not all you were exposed to.

It is no secret that every corner you find liquor, drugs, guns, and more. There was not a day that went by that these were not visible to these kids playing in the streets. Oh how Tony knew his life could have been different if only he could have had the opportunity to play on a team. This is also the reason why he takes such pride in ensuring our son plays on a team, and he can be "that" dad.

Growing up in an environment of poverty would have been difficult for any single parent. With eight kids to feed, his mom provided what she could, but sports leagues and other programs, if available, would have been more than she could manage. So instead, they found contentment playing in the streets.

Father Figures and Friends

> A man of too many friends comes to ruin, But there is a friend who sticks closer than a brother.
>
> —Proverbs 18:24

Tony was not always close with his older brothers, but he did always watch them. Seeking for them to show him what he was not getting from his father. He sought a figure to look up to, but not finding them willing to give him what he needed. Often trying to hang out with them, Tony was pushed away as the annoying little brother.

Realizing today, they were stuck too. They were in the same environment without a father figure present at the time, and they could not give Tony what he was looking for. They are not bad men at heart, and he often talks about them today. They just could not give him what they did not have. This has been hard for Tony to get his head around over the years, but it allows him to forgive and love them where they are at right now.

Quickly understanding that he was the annoying brother, Tony turned to the friends he had in the neighborhood. As Tony grew up, he would have many friends, some he will even still connect with today. From time to time, they call each other and often reminisce about good times and talk about how different their lives are today.

These are great days for Tony as the smile on his face shows how much he values those conversations. Although he had many friends, there was one friend that was like a brother. We will call him Roger, and the two of them were inseparable.

They had a bond and a love for adventure in their friendship. There was not usually someplace you would find one and not the other. As kids, they would have conversations around what they wanted to be when they grew up. One very specific dream that Tony remembers was to be sitting on a porch of a mansion at fifty together with their families and their kids running around playing. They were determined to be friends forever.

This memory is so significant now that his birthday approached. For years, Tony has tried to find out if Roger was still alive and doing well. Although they have not talked, Tony does know Roger is alive and doing well in another city. Tony's prayers for him will continue most likely for the rest of his life, but for now, he is okay with knowing Roger is safe.

Tony's early childhood was filled with so many great memories of adventure, friendship, and the love of his mother. Yet there was a darkness that surrounded the streets, and as you approach adolescence, it calls to you.

Like most things in life, you do not seek trouble. It is not like Tony woke up one day and said I want to go get into trouble. Trouble though was engraved in their environment and the people around them. The thing about the streets is they draw you in. They make promises of freedom, but like the devil, those freedoms come with a cost.

It is not hard to imagine how the streets could draw you in. All around them was brokenness. Tony was surrounded day in and day out with this environment. Many times he would see guns pulled on people over an argument, being witness to chains being snatched off the necks of strangers, or watching the shoes taken off the feet of others. These were not uncommon in these streets on a daily basis.

As fights would break out, a group would gather. Much the same as they do today, and Tony needed to learn how to fight as a way of protecting himself or how to get out of the situation and use his legs to run and not look back.

Tony did not think much of this at the time, but looking back, you can see where they became numb to the environment. Long gone are the voices that told Tony there is better than where he was, and the streets laced with the history of those that came before him were always calling him. The streets called out to with false promises and just like they called the others, they were getting closer to him.

Tony learned to be skeptical of kindness, leery of authority, and how to survive when he felt there was no other way. He watched his mom break her back to raise kids, and Tony wanted more. There were always cops coming around the neighborhood, but there was no trust in them.

When you are young, trouble starts small. It started with Tony and Roger breaking into a school to steal soda from the vending machines. They had thoughts of gym equipment too, but because they were locked away so well, they settled for just the sodas. Soon they heard security and the sirens coming. Anxious they were about to get caught, they quickly grabbed their sodas and got out before the cops could arrive.

The rush of almost getting caught was exhilarating, and it gave them confidence at their ability to get away. Their adventurous spirit was leading them toward trouble and the next rush. They were hooked by the thrill this gave them. Young enough to say it was all just a prank, but the truth was it was just the beginning.

It is that adventurous spirit that led them to next jumping the turnstiles of the subway, so they could explore the world outside of their neighborhood. Every day they would get together and ride the trains to various parts of the city. This was the escape of the norm to see what the world around them had to offer. With no money to pay, they jumped.

After a while, there was not much of the city Tony and Roger did not know. They knew all the nooks and crannies of a busy city, and they flowed through like they belonged. So many times you would find them leaving early in the morning and not returning until later in the evening.

Watching from a distance, Tony learned from his brothers about how to manage the streets. His older brothers had respect and authority, and Tony was intrigued. Tony and Roger were always careful to not be the annoying brothers, but mimicking them at times in their behavior.

There were a few times when trouble first started that Tony would call on his brothers to defend him if things got a little out of hand. They would help from time to time, but they had to learn on their own how to handle their troubles. As Tony would get older, he found himself having to even step in to fight for his older brothers when trouble arrived.

The trouble turns you around. They found themselves getting increasingly bolder. It was a false confidence Tony had in his ability to outrun the cops. Tony was getting away with trouble, and he felt invincible. It festers and it grows, and you become a strong force to be reckoned with. Soon school was not as important, and the adventure of the streets consumed Tony's mind. Soon the fighting increased, and he loved the feeling of control.

Tony soon earned his nickname in the streets. His fearless nature earned him the nickname *Ant Rock*. He had established a reputation of being hard as a rock, and the name stuck. This is what he was known by on the streets, and many from the past still call him today.

As the trouble started, Tony had to face the punishments from his mother, but the streets were strong, and her words were merely seeds. At this point, these punishments would sometimes deter him from bigger trouble, but Tony's desire was growing, and he was a little hardheaded. After all, the streets were freedom, they were adventure; they were calling him and drawing him closer.

As he was getting older, the look of his apartment did too. One of Tony's older brothers was heading to prison for a short while, and his brother's wife and new baby boy were coming to live there. While another one of his older brothers had gone off to the military for a while. Two of Tony's older sisters had gone to school.

What sticks in Tony's mind to this day was seeing his nephew so small and so impressionable without a father there. He loved his aunt and nephew, but there was sadness for them in the situation they were in. It made Tony really start to think about prison and how this was something he did not want in his life. It probably steered him from some trouble, but he didn't get the nickname *Ant Rock* without a reason.

Roger was smart in school while Tony struggled. Roger being so book smart would always protect him and help him pass classes. Roger got the girls as he was smooth, and the ladies loved him while Tony typically got the cousin. They were like brothers, and for that, you always look out for each other. Both were strong and not afraid to jump into a fight and throw a few punches, and together they were feared.

His mom was not crazy about Roger, but mainly because when the two of them were together, they always seemed to find trouble, but to them it was about finding adventure. They were connected by the bond to explore together and discover the outside world.

Adventure is a tricky desire. In one sense, it is not bad to want to explore as that is what teaches us and gives us life's perspective, but adventure can be manipulated with bad choices that create the false sense of power.

Think about where you might be making choices for adventure and ask yourself if what you are choosing to do lines up with what God is teaching you?

Invincible

> Now I urge you, brethren, keep your eye on those who cause dissensions and hindrances contrary to the teaching which you learned, and turn away from them. For such men are slaves, not of our Lord Christ but of their own appetites; and by their smooth and flattering speech they deceive the hearts of the unsuspecting.
>
> —Romans 16:17–18

By the time Tony was sixteen, running the streets was just a part of his life. Desperate for more, Tony and Roger began selling drugs off and on to make some money. Tony knew there was risk, but the ability to have the money was too much to pass up. There was an excitement in this because the money would provide things Tony had not had before.

For the first time, Tony was able to buy nicer shoes that would last longer than a week, able to buy nicer clothes to wear, and he was able to give his mother some money to help her with her bills. It was important for Tony, and although his mother probably knew, she did not always ask where it came from.

The reality is Tony could not shake the lingering feeling that this was playing with fire, and if he got caught, jail would be a real possibility. He was not about to go to jail, so for the next several years, he lived with one eye open and learning to not sell to people you did not know.

Having drugs so easily at your disposal, Tony started experimenting with drugs at this time. Weed was his drug of choice. While so many he knew were getting hooked on heroin and cocaine, Tony never liked how they made him feel, so he chose to leave them alone. It became a regular occurrence to sit and hang out with a group of friends with a blunt to pass around.

Every year in May, birthdays were a big deal as Tony and Roger were only days apart and another friend was right in between. It was like a weeklong celebration for all. They had some good times together on those streets, but the streets were now grabbing hold of them, and their dreams of a better life were getting further and further away.

The nights and weekends were what Tony lived for at that time. They spent time at the movie theater in the city across the bridge smoking weed and drinking their beer. They were rowdy, but they were together, and many steered clear from challenging them.

They spent time scouring all parts of the city and other parts of Brooklyn just to say they could. At night, there would be a small group of them sitting in the projects on the stairs just talking and passing the weed.

They always knew cops would show up in the area, so their eyes were always open. There were many times they have to scatter quickly when the police would show up. The cops knew who they were, sometimes coming to the door looking for Tony. His mom did not trust the cops much then either, so she would help handle the police, but afterwards meant Tony had to deal with his mom.

It took many years, but Tony always knew he deserved his punishments from his mother. His consistent trouble with the cops was edging him closer to jail. Being a single mom, she could not watch him all the time, and she desperately was urging Tony to make different choices and to not follow the patterns of his brothers. Tony though was not always prepared to listen.

Territory was important in the streets. The projects you lived in were yours, and the surrounding projects were a rival of sorts. You did not just go to other projects unless you were looking for trouble, and you especially did not go alone. It was known that when you crossed back into your own projects, you were home, you were safe.

Safe was a relative term when they lived in the streets. It usually meant there was a level of protection you had in the relationships you had around you, but it did not mean you were not looking over your shoulder. If trouble started in your area, word would spread quickly, and before you knew it, others arrived ready to fight.

As teenagers, many of them ran the streets. They controlled their territory, and they were a force to be reckoned with. Everyone knew who they were, and no one dared challenge them. There were not many fights at this time where they would be outnumbered as long as they were in their own territory.

Protection would not just be Tony's, but his family as well. It was one thing to mess with each other, but leave the mothers alone. His mom probably never knew the extent of the protection she had all the years in those projects.

This cycle of running the streets is passed down through the years. As Tony became older, the younger kids in the projects would take over, and the cycle continues. Many of them were little babies when he was in control and are now grown and have taken over. This was survival, this was the streets, and this was his life.

These are the easier stories for him to tell. In the streets, you earn respect, and your loyalty earned you lifelong friends where each of you could understand where you came from. He will tell you that he wished things could have had some different outcomes, but adventure is tricky. If not tamed, it could lead you to choices that lead to trouble. He had to survive, and it was that, or he was a victim of those same streets.

It is easy to say he did not have a choice to live the way he was living, but that would be a lie. There is always a choice, but the temptation of the devil is strong in those streets. Tony had the seeds of God planted in him as a child, but the temptation of the streets was always pulling him in. The mindset that Tony adopted at a young age watching the others in the neighborhood was conqueror or victim.

Tony had been so used to getting away with trouble and the loyalty of the neighborhood that the word *consequences* did not mean anything. He carried a false confidence that says he was not like the others; he was too strong, too hard, and after all, he was the Ant Rock.

Once fighting became a regular occurrence for Tony, he knew it was something he was good at. It felt good for him to throw a few punches. If someone Tony knew was being threatened, he was right there ready to throw a few punches. He was not going to be a victim without a fight, and when he showed up, people paid attention. There was power and control in his fists. It earned him respect and fed his confidence.

To give you a deeper perspective on the power Tony felt he had, there is a story he tells about Halloween. In the projects, Halloween is one of the most dangerous holidays of the year. All the stores will close before dark, and everyone goes inside. This is not a night for trick or treating, candy, and costume parties. It is a night of destruction where others will dress in costumes to cover their faces, put rocks in socks, and run the streets looking to inflict pain.

One Halloween, Tony was out later than normal. He had a girlfriend at the time, and they were walking back after dark. It was just the two of them, and she was terrified because she knew it was late, and the streets were dangerous. Tony however was not fazed by the fear this night held. To him, it was just another night, and he was walking his lady home.

From a distance, they saw them coming. A group of young kids dressed to fully disguise their identities were running toward them with the socks in their hands. She had started to panic, and Tony just put his arm around her shoulder and told her to just keep walking. The group ran right by them as if they were not there, and he finished walking her home.

This was the respect he was given, and the power that he felt he had in the streets. Sadly, when you experience that level of respect, it can make your choices bolder. The power you feel you have puts aside the voices of reason. You are untouchable, and no one can tell you otherwise. The thing about this kind of power though is it makes you blind to things happening around you.

While Tony's mother worked, he was sneaking out to hang in the streets, smoking weed, drinking with his friends, and finding the fights. Tony no longer listened to authority much, and he was living a lifestyle that was blinding him to the consequences he would one day face.

With each bad decision, Tony was getting further from God and always thought he could handle things himself. How many of us live this way today? How many of us try and control our lives and cannot understand why it is falling apart? He was living the lie the streets fed to him, and the lie that he was invincible.

Looking back, he knows the choices Tony was making would ultimately end in pain. He believed the promises of the streets, and his choices were driven by the power he felt to control his own outcome. Things like education and knowledge did not fit into his plan at the time.

How many of us have broken promises? How many of us have made choices based on how we felt and then regretted it later? Lord knows I have, and I had to deal with those consequences. Not because I am bad, but because we push away the wisdom and tried to control our own outcome.

The promise of power from the streets was superficial and could not last. When you are young, that is the hardest part to grasp. Tony felt he was in full control of his life and that no one would dare mess with him. Mess with him no, but ultimately they will move on and do other things, and where will he be?

As you search your heart, look for the areas that you have pushed away wisdom that were given in the words of life spoken around you for the pull of adventure. Where have you pushed away patience for the instant gratification world? Where did you push away grace for others that were struggling?

He was living for the adventure and the excitement. He felt freedom in his ability to run the streets and protect himself. The funny thing about betrayal is it most often comes from the ones that you care about.

It Can't Last Forever

For all have sinned and fall short of the glory of God,

—Romans 3:23, ESV

For several years, this was Tony's life, but at eighteen, his seeds from the past were stirring in him, and he changed one of his choices. Tony was tired of playing with the fire of selling drugs, so, almost as abruptly as he started, he quit selling drugs and sought out to get a regular job.

The money was good, but the risk was too great. Having to always watch over his shoulder was tiring and not how Tony wanted to spend his life. The hardest part of getting a regular job was how the money is so vastly different. At the time, you were lucky if you could make $3.25 an hour, but it was legal, and it kept him out of jail.

It turned out that Tony had a great work ethic. The seeds his mom sowed definitely paid off. He worked hard and was always reliable. Maybe it was his deep desire to not want any handouts in life, or maybe it was just the strong feeling of accomplishment. He gave 100 percent in the jobs Tony had and making his own money to help his mom and to take care of his own needs were very important aspects in his life.

Tony was young and held a few different jobs during those few years. Each he seemed to enjoy, but needing to make more money, he would move on. He was a boy moving into early manhood, and the money was necessary if he wanted to move on from the apartment in a few years.

Tony's lifestyle had not changed much outside of getting a job. He still looked forward to hanging out on the streets with his friends drinking and passing the blunt. Life was changing though. They were getting older, and a series of events was about to shift his life in a completely different direction.

Being second to youngest of eight children meant Tony's mother was starting to get older. Tony was nearing twenty years old, and his mother was nearing retirement. She had started having some health battles with her blood pressure, and the stress of work was proving to be too much.

Over the last several years, the look of the apartment continued to change. Tony's brother in the military had returned home because of medical issues; while his oldest brother had moved to Pennsylvania. Tony's brother that was in prison was now home, and his sisters had returned from school.

After some issues, his aunt moved out with his nephew, and one of his sisters was expecting his new nephew "T" while Tony and his little brother were just starting to reach manhood. As Tony's mother neared retirement, she was ready to leave the city and move to Pennsylvania closer to the oldest son and a quieter place to live.

His mother's decision to put the two older sisters in charge of the apartment when she moved was not a popular one, but Tony's mother knew she needed to put it into the hands of the two that would ensure lights stayed on and life would carry on when she was gone. So, despite the objections from all the boys, the decision was made.

Around the same time, Tony had gotten word that some drivers for a large beverage company were always looking for help, and the money was better than the hourly wage he was making. He had been told to go to the yard in Queens and ask the drivers if they needed help. If they needed it and could afford it, they would take you. So, one morning, he showed up and was surprised that he was immediately able to connect with a driver for the day.

It was day work, so work ethic would be a key if you wanted to keep working. These drivers needed people who would be reliable and work hard. If you worked hard, they would take you again, but if you didn't, you got paid for the day but not likely to continue on. Like in most companies, word spreads, so if you failed with one driver, your reputation would carry to the others.

That first day, Tony impressed his driver with his ability to work. This driver recognized that he was willing to work hard and loved that about him. Although he could not afford him every day, when the workday was over, the driver told Tony he would make sure he always had work on a truck even if not with him.

As long as Tony would keep showing up and working hard, the drivers in return would make sure he always had a driver to go out with. He loved this setup and he loved the work, so every day he showed up, and as promised, every day he went out on a truck.

As Tony hit twenty years old, he was about to really hit manhood. Manhood is something every boy must enter at some point. How you enter though is one thing he never considered. He had made some choices to change some things in his life, but past choices were about to catch up to him, and the consequences would be the beginning of a three-year spiral he never saw coming.

At home, Tony's mother was preparing to move, and so was his little brother. This would leave his three sisters, two older brothers, his youngest nephew, and himself in the apartment. He worked through the day on the trucks, got off work to get his weed and his alcohol to hang out for a while, and he would go home to sleep. This was his daily routine, and he was content for now as he started thinking about being able to be out on his own.

Tony's job was going very well. He was now splitting time between four drivers and working every day during the week. There was one particular driver he was going out with more frequently, and he calls him Frenchy. He was a little older than the other drivers, and he was about to purchase his route fully. Frenchy kept talking to the others about taking Tony full-time. The others resisted because they relied on him during their heaviest days, so for a period of time, Tony split his week with the four drivers.

A short time after Frenchy completed the purchase of his route, he came to Tony and without hesitation told him he was going to work with Frenchy full-time. He didn't mind because he liked Frenchy, and he was just happy to go to work every day. The others were disappointed but did not fight Frenchy as they knew they could not afford to keep Tony as much as they would like. So from that point on, he started working directly with Frenchy.

Frenchy had his own family at home outside the city and had busted his butt to get this route all to himself. He was a good boss and would encourage him to do more. Frenchy did not slack on you either. He was stern when needed and even sometimes would yell at him to get his attention. Not something we often appreciate, but Tony was young, and he needed some discipline.

In the city, you had to know the customers, sell the product, unload the truck, arrange it on shelves, and collect the money. It was an all-around job for one truck. If you were good, you did not lack work to keep you busy, and Frenchy was good at his job.

Frenchy took Tony under his wing and showed him the ropes. He learned how to load, how to sell the product, how to collect the money. Many times Frenchy sent him across to another stop to collect money while Frenchy finished up the stop they were on. Frenchy gave him trust and in return he got loyalty.

The thought crossed Tony's mind a few times after collecting and holding so much money to just take it and not look back, but they were short-lived thoughts, and he never did. He respected Frenchy and was not about to steal from him. As time went on, Frenchy trusted him more and more with the money and the purchases, and Tony was happy to do it.

It wasn't until years later that Tony fully understood just how God brought Frenchy into his life. In so many ways, he was more than a boss. Frenchy took care of him like a son. He yelled at him when he needed it, he taught him, he fed him, and he was the male figure he so desperately needed in his life. After twenty years of life, he had finally found the father figure he had been searching for.

Now that Tony was working full-time, his friendship with Roger had started to grow apart. The path they were on was different. He still loved his friend and enjoyed seeing Roger, but less and less their paths crossed.

Tony's home life was also different. With his mother gone, he established himself a simple routine of working and hanging out which left him out of the apartment much of the time. He was being fed at work, and the money he had been making helped with the rest. He was oblivious to the life happening in his home and what was happening when he was not there.

To talk about the rest, you need his perspective now from the Bible. At some point in our lives, we are all hurt or betrayed. Sometimes hurt by those that are closest to us, and life can seem so unfair.

If we go back for a moment, we can see betrayal and hurt when you look at the story of Jesus and the cross. How a perfectly innocent man was betrayed by someone close to him, how he suffered at the hands of others, he was beaten and forced to carry a cross to his death for doing nothing wrong. Yet despite all of this, he loved and went on to save us all.

Tony's choices did not make him innocent, but betrayal still occurs. He was not free of sin, and the life he was living was far from perfect. Trust may waiver and your heart broken, but forgiveness is freedom. After all, three days later, Jesus rose from the dead and through his blood we are here today.

Tony still remembers the hot July afternoon when the darkness first showed up. He had just finished working and was heading home for a shower and a nap. Hot and tired, he arrived at the apartment only to find that his sisters had changed the locks.

His sisters had decided without him that it was time to go, and so with no warning, no discussion, no deadlines, no notice, they changed the locks and put him on the street.

Nowhere to Turn

For the Son of Man came to seek and to save the lost.

—Luke 19:10

The betrayal Tony felt from his family was indescribable. The pain and the hurt quickly turned to anger. How could they just put him on the street? Whatever happened to discussing the intent and what needed to happen? What happened to giving Tony time to find another place to live? He was not given this courtesy, and his anger boiled over.

Here Tony was twenty years old and homeless. His anger was now front and center, and his feelings of abandonment and betrayal had boiled to the surface. He yelled at his sisters when they announced what they had done. Not finding them willing to reconsider, his anger grew, and he walked away.

How had Tony been so blind to not see this coming? He knew his life choices were not the best, but who gets to decide your fate in this way without even a warning. His choices and feelings of invincibility had caught up with him, and he never expected to feel betrayed and abandoned by his family.

Tony had been drinking and smoking weed daily with his friends, but now he turned to alcohol and weed to attempt to drown the pain and anger he felt. He had no place to go, and the streets that had often called his name were now his home. He was powerless to his sisters' decisions to kick him out since his mother did turn the apartment over to them.

The betrayal Tony felt extended beyond the family during these days. He was in his projects, he was in his territory, and oh how quickly your protection from the others you know would be gone. He was alone and with no place to turn; he found himself a prisoner to his mind and his anger.

His first night on the streets would be the beginning of a long stretch of destructive patterns. Some would even probably say Tony was at rock-bottom of his life. Tony may have been homeless and alone, but he was not ready to change, so his spiral would continue.

With nowhere to go, Tony went up to the roof and looked over at the streets. Through the night, he would see lights in the windows go on and off and gradually as the night wore on, the streets would empty, and he would be all alone. The view from the roof made him feel that even though many had very little, they all had a roof over their head except for him.

At night, the alcohol and drugs were meant to drown the pain, but instead just enhanced his anger and aided in his feelings that there was nothing left for him in this world. Have you ever been so angry you just wanted to hit something? Imagine living with that feeling day in and day out. Tony's world had crumbled with just one action, and he was quickly spiraling out of control.

As Tony's anger turned to rage, he would search the streets looking for a fight. He was looking for someone or something to punish for the situation he was in. If you were in his path and often alone, you would be his target. Not enough to kill anyone, but enough for them to feel his pain. He was lost and had nothing to lose, so his anger at his family came out on other people.

Sleep became scarce. If Tony was lucky, he might get an hour or two a night. This fueled by the drugs and alcohol meant many nights wandering the streets, or spent looking for the next fight made sleep almost nonexistent. When he finally had enough for the night, he would go find a rooftop or a bridge and wait for the dawn to break the darkness. This was Tony's hope of a new day, and he would rise with the sun and head to work.

Tony was living almost two different lives. At night he was alone and succumbed to the thoughts in his mind, his anger, and the lies of the alcohol. When the sun would rise, he would go to work where he knew he had food, acceptance, and a small glimpse of hope. Not knowing where to turn, he just wandered the streets until it was time to work.

After his first night on the street, he pulled himself together and headed to work. He needed to tell Frenchy about his situation as he would not be able to hide it by his appearance. Knowing the truth could mean that he no longer had the job with Frenchy. Not so much because he was homeless, but because he was desperate and that could lead to problems.

God was staying present in Tony's life during this time. Despite how his nights were, God was still seeking him. Frenchy was not happy with the truth Tony was telling him, but despite the change, Frenchy decided to keep him working. The blessing of Frenchy was a man would never give up on him.

Why would he continue to help this young man that was just a straight mess? Maybe it was the relationship they had built, or maybe it was Tony's good work ethic. Either way, Frenchy was a small light of hope in a very dark world.

I can imagine it was pretty hard at times as Tony had no place to shower or clean up. Many times rolling into work smelling like death warmed over. Tony would be reeking of alcohol, hung over, and bruised from the night before, but he would arrive every day ready to work.

Frenchy would always make sure he got something to eat right away, and after eating, they would head to work for the day. As this was day work, each day Frenchy would pay Tony for the day, and much to Frenchy's dismay, Tony took little bit of cash and sought the medicine for his pain.

The workday would end, and once again his loneliness overcame him. Tony does not remember fully how, but he had gotten word that his father was in North Carolina. He had little to no relationship with him through the years, but he found a way to contact him, and his father agreed to let him come stay. So, in a last-ditch effort, Tony left Frenchy and sought out his father for help.

The degree of separation is so small when it comes to how quickly life can change. Each person may not have had his experiences, but in your own experiences, where has life changed suddenly and where did you turn? When you look back, can you see where God was knocking and trying to get your attention?

Two Hard Hearts

> The Lord passed before him and proclaimed, "The Lord, the Lord, a God merciful and gracious, slow to anger, and abounding in steadfast love and faithfulness, keeping steadfast love for thousands, forgiving iniquity and transgression and sin, but who will by no means clear the guilty, visiting the iniquity of the fathers on the children and the children's children, to the third and the fourth generation.
>
> —Exodus 34:6–7

When Tony arrived in North Carolina, he very quickly learned that his time with his father would not last. He was not welcomed with open arms and love of a father. He was welcomed almost as an obligation where his father quickly laid down the law of how things would be.

Tony's father did not talk about what he had been up to or how he could change. The law laid down said it all. He was not thrilled about these rules, but to be out of the streets for a while meant sacrifice.

His father had turned to ministry and was the pastor in a small church. Tony's father would take him to church with him every day. He remembers sometimes going to the church just to go to the church. His father had found his salvation and felt a calling to share with others, but that did not teach him how to be a father.

It was not so much the rules Tony's father laid down, or the days of having to follow his father like a child that bothered him as much as the fact that Tony did not know this man and his father did not really know him. Both of their hearts were hardened by life and experience, and communication was not either of their strong suit.

Tony was full of questions for the five-year-old that did not understand why his dad left. He had many questions as to why his father would leave his mother to raise eight kids on her own. How could his father have faith in God and not help his family?

Tony's father was hard to live with; something his mother had warned him about many years ago. His father was a loner and liked being alone. His father's rules, his father's hardness were only damaging an anger-fueled heart further.

Finally to a point where Tony really wanted some answers, he sat down to talk with his father. What he recalls of that conversation left him with more questions than answers started when he asked his father:

"Why are you alone?"

"It is God's will."

"That does not make sense. Do you want to be alone for the rest of your life?"

"If that is God's will."

"Daddy, no one should die alone. Why would you leave a woman you had eight children with? Why not make something work?"

"We just didn't get along, and she wanted me gone."

"But you left Mommy to break her back to raise all of us kids, why?"

"She wanted me gone."

At this point, Tony gave up going any further. None of the answers his father provided seemed to provide peace and closure. Over the years, he would ask again with very little success. Like him, his father had locked those pieces away and continuing to ask seemed pointless.

In the Bible, it talks about the sins of the father carry over. His father learned from his father, and the pattern was established. Tony's father knew how to do many things, but he never knew how to be a father, so he had nothing to give his own children. It is not an excuse but an understanding you gain with time.

The good news comes later in the Bible despite the sins and patterns of our fathers, we are the children of God, and those patterns can be broken. When you turn your eyes to the true father, you can be redeemed. This life we have been given may seem good or bad, but God will always use our situations for good.

Tony may not have known much of his father then, but as Tony became a father himself, he understood that his father must have suffered a lot of pain in his life just as Tony was suffering through his situation.

So, after just three short months, Tony had enough of this situation and purchased a bus ticket back home. Knowing he still would have no place to go but knowing he could not stay where he was, he accepted that he was going back to the streets alone.

The choice Tony made to go back to the streets instead of sticking it out with his father was a hard one to make. Looking back, he had no regrets for leaving. He was not moving forward, and having two hard hearts in one place was difficult. Let's face it, both needed healing, but they were not going to find it in each other. Like most twenty-year-olds, you think you are better off alone, and you can find your own way out of trouble.

Tony arrived back into New York just as winter was beginning. Clothed in only jeans, sneakers, and a T-shirt, it was a miracle he did not freeze to death. He does not remember feeling the cold, but most of the time he was drunk or high.

At times drudging through the snow to get from place to place and looking for somewhere to keep warm, he found the trains to ride just to stay warm. Having not showered and wreaking of alcohol, most people just ignored him while he sat on the train.

Many times Tony remembers being on the train just riding it until it stopped. The warmth of the train kept him from freezing, and one day he dozed off. Tired, Tony slept through until there was silence. The train had stopped, and he was stunned to realize they were in Coney Island. Not really expecting to go this far, he hopped off and waited for the train that would take him back to the city.

It is about survival and doing what you can. It is not about living life, but existing through each day. Tony was cold, he was tired, and he was hungry, and hope was just a pipe dream to him. Looking for resources to get through the days, he called on Frenchy.

Frenchy did not hesitate to welcome Tony back to work, and to Frenchy, he was happy just to see Tony alive. Tony was grateful that he had this man that always welcomed him, taught him, and cared for him.

Each night at the end of their day, Frenchy would always tell him to get out of the streets. The streets would kill him if he did not get out. Tony appeased Frenchy, and deep down he knew Frenchy was right but did not know how, so his cycle continued.

Tony found himself full of shame on how he had fallen so far. The young invincible kid was now for the most part alone. He had Frenchy during the day, but the reality that this was his boss and not his father was difficult to swallow sometimes. The time with Tony's father left him almost as broken as when he arrived.

Night after night, the reels would play over and over in Tony's mind. You are not worthy, no one wants you, and how does everyone seem to have a home except you? Night after night when he was alone, he began to contemplate life altogether.

Who wouldn't? The only thing Tony knew was the situation he was in. He did not think about his future. He did not dare to dream that there would be a family of his own one day. All he could think about is how far he had fallen, and salvation seemed so far out of his reach. The devil was working overtime just to keep him down. He was falling into the devil's grasp, and the devil wanted him to finish the task.

The devil comes to your mind and feeds you the lies, and in the absence of truth, you believe the lie. Tony's anger was feeding the evil in his heart, and the reels were playing over and over in his head and driving him crazy. No amount of alcohol or weed could stop the reels; no matter how many times he fought, he could not shake the reels. He was lost, and life was dark.

It had almost been a year, and he was still on the streets. The only light in his darkness was the job he held. Now, it may seem like that is not much, but it was more than he could have hoped for, and more than he certainly deserved.

Just like his friend today, there are so many in the pits of despair where the devil plays in your mind. How many of us have felt this lost? We may have pushed God so far to the backburner that the only voices we heard are the devil. Just because we have pushed God back does not mean he is not there. Just because we are lost does not mean God will not help you. When was the last time you asked God for help?

Sleeping Among Enemies

> The thief comes only to steal and kill and destroy; I have come that they may have life, and have it to the full.
>
> —John 10:10

What place do you go to and contemplate life? Tony's was often a rooftop or a bridge in the city where he would find himself at 3:00 a.m. Drunk, angry, and homeless every night. When the city slept, he did not. How many times did he consider jumping and just giving up on it all?

Night after night, the crazy thoughts would run through Tony's head, but when it came to the decision to jump, what seemed as illogical reasons was intervention from God. In all his thoughts to jump, he would just keep thinking about making Frenchy mad if he was late for work. Thinking about what kind of headache he would have for days. Tony knew jumping would kill him, but the thought of letting Frenchy down stopped him from jumping.

Even in his most broken state, God was protecting him. The smallest of lights in a world of darkness can sometimes be the difference in your decisions. It did not change his situation at that time, but it was enough to keep him alive night after night and moving forward.

Why would God want Tony, what was he worth? There was no logical reason for his thoughts, but God used it to get his attention. God whispered something he would hear to prevent him from ending his life. God was not done with Tony yet, and God kept the light shining in the darkness to get Tony through until he was ready.

Tony did not understand the logic, and every night the urge would be so strong and so powerful, yet it was a whisper of life that kept him going. It was a war of good and evil that raged in Tony night after night on those bridges and rooftops. God used the little light he had to keep the darkness from fully consuming him.

What must it be like to not have any place to really go after work? So many times I dread getting up for work. The never-ending routine of life that is going to work, paying the bills, sleep, and repeat can seem boring. It is honestly part of your day to day, but imagine if that was all gone and all you had was the job? Imagine for a moment that you got up to go to work, and when your shift was done, you had no place to go and rest your head? Imagine not being able to cook a good meal? Imagine your only joy came from when it was time to go to work?

Weekends were especially hard on Tony because those were times he had no work to go to. He still knew many people in the projects and would often wander around to hang out with some of them from time to time. After a year of being on the streets, night after night, most people tended to just steer clear.

The fallout with Roger was no different. Roger had not been around while Tony was in the street. One night as he wandered the streets, he saw Roger with a few other guys hanging out. Tony was excited to see his friend. He tried to approach him. It was clear that Roger was not as excited to see him. Roger turned Tony away and told him to get away. This made Tony angry, and he started yelling at Roger demanding to know what was up with him.

Roger did not want to explain to Tony why he was pushing him away. After all, the man before Roger was drunk, he was angry, and he was not the same person he called friend all these years. Angry Roger lashed back saying he was going to kick Tony's butt if he didn't leave him alone. Roger was not ready for the confrontation and knew he would not be heard if he did say something. So instead, Roger pushed Tony away and threatened to fight him when he did not leave.

To Tony, this was just another betrayal. Why would he expect less? Angry and hurt, Tony just spread his arms, and raising his chest, he invited Roger to try to fight him. He had nothing to lose, and Roger knew it. Tony's anger was to a point where he was even ready to fight his best friend. Before anything could go further, Roger just walked away, and Tony retreated to his pattern more hurt and broken than before.

It would be many years before Tony would see Roger again, and there was a sadness that this lifelong friendship was coming to an end. This end meant it was taking with it all the dreams they had as kids of growing old together as friends.

Today, Tony will tell you he does not blame Roger. Tony was dangerous and in an out-of-control spiral with his anger. He was not a friend to Roger when Roger needed it and could not expect his friend would want to be around someone that was so destructive at the time, but when you are living in that darkness, there is so much pain in feeling abandoned by the ones you loved.

Being in the streets, Tony became somewhat resourceful. After coming back from North Carolina, he had met a young lady in one of the rival projects. Not the best place for Tony to be, but when she told him he could stay there for five dollars a day, he did not want to pass that up.

This meant he would have to sleep in the presences of his enemies, but nothing about Tony seemed to care. Besides, when you are desperate for a place to sleep, you are willing to pay with both money and the consequences that may come.

This agreement did not come without issues. She lived in an apartment where people went to get high. Every day and through the night, there would be people coming in and out with one main purpose. Tony was out of place, and they all knew it.

The majority of the people coming in and out did not like Tony being there, and he did not care. Each of them already altered by the drugs they were consuming just made the situation more difficult.

He was already willing to die on the streets; he had already abandoned his hope for the future, so at the time, nothing anyone would throw at him would shake him.

Being in this environment meant quite a few fights over the time Tony stayed with her. Oftentimes with individuals, but a few times with smaller groups of people. It probably would have been worse, but he worked during the day and would wander at night before going to rest, so it was a small price to pay so he could sleep. It certainly could not last this way, but it was a solution for now.

He was in a no-win situation. Staying in the streets at night meant no sleep, and only the reels playing in his head or to have a bed to sleep in surrounded by other drug addicts that wanted nothing more than to have him gone and destroyed. Tony had to fight just to rest his head no matter the situation he was in.

Finding his situation becoming increasingly difficult, his light grew one afternoon after work when he noticed his brother Allen in the area.

There are so many questions that surround me as I sit to help Tony put these events into words. All the pieces about how territory was important and you were safe when you crossed back into your neighborhood were merely lies the devil played in your mind. How was it that his own neighborhood left him on the street and yet he found shelter amongst his enemies?

Many times I think we look at territory as our safe place, and maybe it is holding you back. Maybe your comfort zone keeps you from seeing what truly may be going on. Is it time to examine your situation for the pieces you may have been blind to? Have you become like Tony and are actually sleeping among enemies? It may be time to get help.

Not Alone

> For in the day of trouble he will keep me safe in his dwelling; he will hide me in the shelter of his sacred tent and set me high upon a rock.
>
> —Psalm 27:5

Tony had heard that Allen was also in the streets. Allen had been put out by his sisters, but Tony had not seen him until now. They talked for a while, and Allen explained that he was staying out there with a girlfriend that he met right after being thrown out. They had found a place on the other side of the bridge in an old abandoned building. It was not much, but it was a roof over their heads.

This caught Tony's attention. He had been having issues in the other apartment, and he knew he needed to make a change. Tony asked more questions and asked him if he could go with Allen to this building. His brother's response was an immediate no.

Allen explained that his girlfriend did not want him to stay. Maybe that was an excuse, but either way, it just fueled Tony's anger. Why would Allen come to see Tony and tell him about this place? Why would his brother pick his girlfriend over family? Tony's frustration boiled over, and after yelling at Allen, they went their separate ways.

Much to Tony's surprise, his brother Allen returned the next day to find him hanging out. They argued for a few minutes, but

Allen determined to reconcile asked Tony to come stay with him and apologized for the night before. This was his brother, and he was offering Tony an opportunity to get away from the apartment he had been staying in. Reluctantly, Tony agreed, and he set off to make one last stop for weed and beer, and they hopped on the train.

As they approached, the building was dark. It was in an almost forgotten part of the city, and it was a sight to see. Here stood an old broken building that was many stories tall, and the building was filled with other homeless people. The building sat next to a park that was also filled with other homeless people.

At that moment, Tony realized that he had never seen so many homeless people like him in one place. Each had their little space living their lives. Up until that point, his view from the rooftop had convinced him he was the only one living on the streets. The lie he had believed that nobody else suffered his same fate. Now Tony is standing there looking upon this park and building and understanding that he was not alone.

As Tony walked through the building, he remembers the shock of some of the things he would see. It was a community of broken people that, like him, had nothing to lose. They were all fiercely protective over their space, and doors did not matter. You left them alone, and they would leave you alone, but once you left, they would gladly take your space. After all, they just wanted a roof over their heads too.

Tony's brother Allen and his girlfriend had a small area in the building. The two of them had found a mattress to sleep on and offered to share some of the space with him. In a small way, it was a reminder of when he was very young living in an old rundown building and sleeping on the floor of a living room. Only this time, there was a mattress. It was not much, but Tony was with family, and he had a roof over his head. It was not a large light, but now with Frenchy, Tony's light was getting bigger.

Allen and his girlfriend had a system they created to keep someone in the space so they would not lose their spot. His girlfriend worked at making that space seem a little like a home and was not afraid to ward off any that might come and try and take the spot.

This made it easier for Tony to get up and go to work knowing he would have this place to return to.

At night, Tony would wander the building going floor to floor. Walking in those halls, he would see people hooking up sexually with no regard for doors or people watching. He would see others shooting up drugs along with a few other things he did not care to mention. It was unlike anything Tony had ever seen.

Looking around, all of these other people were just doing what they knew to survive. They had little hope, and they did not know any other way to be. Tony did not know their stories, but he didn't have to.

Many of them did not have jobs, and Tony would see them at times on the streets holding signs. They were just trying to make enough money for the day, and he realized he had too much pride to ever do this. Thankfully, God knew that and had given him Frenchy, and he did not have to beg for money. The money he made working for Frenchy he mostly purchased alcohol and weed, so it did not leave much for food, so he often found himself hungry.

Thinking back on this today, Tony knows this is why he has a heart for people in his situation. He did not have to hold the sign, but he knows why people do. If he did not have Frenchy, he very well may have needed to do the same thing just to survive day to day.

A thought occurs to him though, he was working and yet he was so fueled with anger and sadness he was stuck. Tony was working and making money, but he needed help. Often he has seen on social media how people are caught driving nice cars and begging for money on the street, and you become hesitant to help others, but all you see is them being caught. We do not know the whole story, and it is easy to judge.

How many times do we just walk by and ignore them? We pretend we do not see them, and we often keep moving. How many times do we curse them for being there claiming that we work hard for our money, or we have a family to support? As Tony learned from his life, the line between people and the homeless is thin. This is why he gives back to those without question. This is why you will see him give people money, food, and clothes.

It takes a special kind of desperation to sit there through such a pride-swallowing experience as begging for money. What must be going on in the lives of those that do have cars that they would even want to sit out there for money? Is it possible they are empty and just trying to hang on to what little they do have?

I have seen studies that show that most homeless people sitting on the street will average around $20–$30 a day. If they were lucky, a little more and that equates to no more than $200 a week, but that would also mean they sit there seven days a week. So, knowing this, you must know that anyone that has a cell phone, or a car, or seemingly regular people that are out there begging are in some kind of a desperate need that we do not know anything about.

All the people in this building were desperate for something. The people Tony knew in the projects were desperate for something. Maybe you are looking for a promotion, maybe you are looking for a job, maybe you have had several failed relationships, or maybe your finances are in a struggle. We all are desperate for something.

That desperation only has one thing in common; it comes from the enemy. It is the one that made us false promises and would rather see us down than seek the one that can change us from the inside out and redeem us. Tony was no different. He was desperate like all the others in his building.

Tony's light may have grown, but his lifestyle had not changed much. He still went to work during the day and still would drink and smoke weed to drown his pain at night. He still looked for fights and still would find himself on the rooftops or bridges to contemplate life. He would spend most of his time drunk or high, but he had now been on the streets homeless for over two years. He had no expectation his life would ever change.

He was tired, plain and simple, just tired. Not just physically tired, but emotionally and spiritually on empty. Tony's gas tank was flashing on the *E*, and he had nothing to refuel it. The words of Frenchy telling him to get out of the streets echoed in his mind. He did not know how, but he was desperately seeking change. Tony's relationship with his brother Allen was not bad, but neither of them had nothing really to give. It is the being on empty and fueled by only Tony's anger left little in the way of productive relationships.

It is not lost on Tony that in the over two years on the streets, no one had not come to really seek him out. It wasn't until Allen sought Tony two years in that he had seen any family member. Tony felt angry that his mother moved and seemingly forgot about him. He was angry he had other brothers he did not see. Why were him and Allen out there when everyone else seemed to be fine? At this point in his life, he was not prepared to really confront how the anger in him was driving everyone away.

Looking back now, Tony knows that his feelings of being abandoned drove his anger, and his anger drove his choices. Tony's heart had been hardened by his situation and his environment. He could not see that the others around him were just as hurt and broken as he was, so it was easy to blame everyone else.

Trust does not come easily for him, but over the years, he has learned through his faith about forgiveness and healing. This is why regardless of how outgoing he is, how social he may be, how he will be a great person to talk to, you may only know the person he is today.

The abandoned building was not much, but it became a home, and Tony was with family. For six months they had been together walking through their situations together. He did not get along to well with Allen's girlfriend, but it did not matter they were together. It felt good to have others in Tony's life. They were not in a great situation, but it was nice to not be lonely every night.

Tired or not, Tony trudged forward, but the dawn was about to break the darkness. His light would grow once again and in his path would come a light he did not know existed. God was working in his life.

God was showing him he was not alone, God was putting people in his path, and God was keeping him alive. Tony may have had a hardened heart, but God was slowly breaking him down and opening his eyes.

Just as said in Jeremiah 29:11: "For I know the plans I have for you, declares the Lord, Plans for welfare and not for calamity to give you a future and a hope."

The whispers of saving were getting stronger. In Tony's tired and weakest state, he had given a way for God to help him and to hear more clearly. If he wanted out, he had to make changes. He may not know fully how, but he knew he had to do something. The words of life spoken into him by Frenchy were surfacing, and he knew something would eventually give.

There was a confusion Tony had as to why he would still be alive. There were so many times over the last two years that he should have died. Whether it was at the hands of someone else, at his own accord on those bridges or rooftops, or just simply freezing to death, he found that in all of this, he was still there.

When Tony was younger, that may have caused a confidence of invincibility, but after two years on the streets and the loss of so much in his life, it was more of a confusion that came. Tony did not understand why he was still there or what was in store, but each day as the sun rose in the sky, he would push forward.

The Hope in Desperation

> He is a merciful creditor, not keeping the items given as security by poor debtors. He does not rob the poor but instead gives food to the hungry and provides clothes for the needy.
>
> —Ezekiel 18:7

One night while in their space of the abandoned building, Allen came walking in with his hands filled with groceries. Surprise would be an understatement as Tony saw Allen walking in the door. Where did this come from? Tony was eager to find out, but more eager to have food to eat. The three of them sat there, pried open a can of beans, and slowly cooked it with a lighter. Once they were fed, Tony asked his brother how he was able to get the food to eat.

It turns out his brother Allen was pretty resourceful. Allen's wandering was not fueled by anger, but by desperation to have food. He had come upon information about a lady named Diane and her ministry that would feed the homeless a few days a week. When she was able, she would also provide a few groceries to feed them in between her visits.

Allen had sought her and talked with her; he was fed and given food to take home. To this point, Tony's life had been so fueled by anger that he had been kept from seeing there was more help out available, and he didn't know it existed. As his brother talked about this ministry, Tony knew he had to go. Her next day coming was Saturday, and he made the plan to go with his brother.

Tony's first encounter with Diane did not go as planned. Not having to work, he stayed out all night drinking, and when Tony went off with his brother to the food line, he was drunk and hungry. Diane liked knowing who she was serving, and so she would talk to each person. Seeing the condition Tony was in, she knew immediately he was drunk, and he was removed from the line. If Tony wanted food, he had to be sober. He was hungry and his choice to keep drinking got him no food.

Tony once again exploded with anger as he began yelling at her. Spouting out things about how he did not need her or her stinking food as he stormed off to drink more. The problem was Tony was hungry and if he wanted to eat, he was going to have to toe the line. He was desperate to eat, so, swallowing his pride, he made up his mind and decided to try again in a few days, only this time he would not drink or get high until after he was fed.

First impressions are often hard to overcome, and truthfully no one would blame her if she turned Tony away after his outburst the last time. Diane though was different. She had a heart for the homeless, and after years of experience, she knew about outbursts. This time he showed up sober and determined to eat.

Tony stood in line as they handed out tickets for the food line and waited his turn. Like usual, Diane talked to each person, and this time noticing he returned sober, her words were more welcoming. She allowed him to stand in line, and she talked with him.

She had learned Allen was Tony's brother and that they had been in the streets for a long time. She was oddly easy to talk to, and after Tony was fed and heading home, he knew he needed to go back.

She was different, and Tony knew it. She did not judge him or hold a grudge. It felt like a plan to just get food when in reality it was so much more. Her authority over that line got Tony to respect someone of authority in order to get what he wanted, but what he did not know at the time was what else this was doing inside of him.

Once again, Tony's desire for not wanting handouts was burning in him. He did not like going there for food and expecting it just to be given to him. His job was a lifeline for him so he did not have to beg for money. So why would he be so keen on standing in a line for free food? Desperate and hungry, he went back a few more times. Each time sober, and each time in conversation with Diane, and she made sure he was being fed not just literally but spiritually.

After a few weeks of going to the food line and talking with Diane, Tony and Allen started showing up early to help with the food line and serving the others. Each time they left fed, and the sense of earning their food. Tony got to meet a few others working in the ministry, and he was grateful to help. This was something new, and they enjoyed doing the task almost as much as they liked having the food in their stomachs.

Since Allen's girlfriend would often stay back at the abandoned building protecting the space, they ensured they always brought food back to eat. During the times in between the ministry coming, they had established a routine. Tony would get up and go to work, and when he came back, food would be waiting for him.

There was a sense that things were improving. They were not out of the streets, but they now had food to keep them strong, and the power of God was moving in their lives. To some this may not seem like much at all, but with each encounter, life was being spoken into Tony. With each encounter, he earned food, and the reward was no hunger. With each encounter, his light was growing, and the little tinges of hope would creep in.

In 2016, it was reported that there were 564,708 homeless people in America and of that in New York, it was reported that just over 61,000 were in the city. Sadly, over 20,000 of them were children. Programs like Diane's do exist, but they cannot possibly reach them all. They do not have the money or the resources. Knowing this, it is all humans' responsibility to help where they can. Where can you help?

The Last Fight

The Lord is not slow in keeping his promise, as some understand slowness. Instead he is patient with you, not wanting anyone to perish, but everyone to come to repentance.

—2 Peter 3:9

Tony had lived for so long with nothing to lose and no desire to accept handouts. His heart had been so hard, he punished himself and others with his fists. He will tell you that at the time it did not feel like not a lot was going to change, but God knew things were changing. Tony's weakness was opening a door for more to be let in. He was almost ready to be saved, but he would have to face some tough decisions to get there.

Other than work, the food line was the only time in the week Tony would be sober and clearheaded. Oftentimes heading straight from the food line to get his daily dose of alcohol and drugs. The light was growing, and he now had a purpose to stay sober for more than just his job.

As part of her ministry, Diane gave out cards with her number so anyone who needed could reach out to her and get ministered to. She gave them out to people in her line in hopes of reaching some. People would politely take it and so did Tony, placing it in his back pocket as he stood for food. He did not give it much thought as she did help them get food and prayer, but she was not out there with them so how could she possibly help further?

God called this woman to serve others. There is really no other explanation for her consistency other than obedience. Like clockwork, she was there to care for those in the streets. Those in the streets came to rely on her being there often arriving early and forming the line even before the vans showed up to prepare. Many of us never fully comprehend the sacrifice or the tenacity it takes to love people right where they are at and just give them kindness, food, a little hope, and most importantly prayer.

> If you give some of your own food to [feed] those who are hungry and to satisfy [the needs of] those who are humble, then your light will rise in the dark, and your darkness will become as bright as the noonday sun. (Isaiah 58:10)

Tony found joy in helping the others in the line. It came to be something he looked forward to rather than feeling desperate for food. He liked feeling as though despite his circumstances, he was able to serve others. He became very good at managing the line of people and getting to know people in the crowd.

Tony now had two people in his life that for no reason at all were genuinely interested in his wellbeing and the wellbeing of his family. Part of the reason he had no regrets in leaving his father's is the view he has from the rearview mirror. Had he stayed with his father, he would have never run into his brother Allen that ultimately led him to Diane and may not have found salvation and a relationship with God.

He always knew that Allen would eventually move on. After all, he had his girlfriend and he was alone and his experience in life taught him that everyone leaves. Only this time, he wanted his brother to provide a better life for himself and his girlfriend. He encouraged Allen to do more and get her out of there. Allen's girlfriend, now pregnant with their first child, was a wakeup call, and when his brother was able to get a job out near Long Island, he knew he had to go.

See, Allen was not alone, and he needed to care for his impending family. Whereas Tony was alone and had pretty much been alone for going on three years. He only had himself to care for which was part of his survival mechanism. Tony had no doubt he would survive alone again. Now it wasn't as though it was joyful to be alone again, but this time there was peace.

His brother Allen and his girlfriend packed up and left the abandoned building for their new life. Without the protector of the space, Tony would lose his spot in the building when he went to work, and once they had gone, his life returned to the normal patterns, and he found himself back at the ladies apartment once again needing a bed and once again sleeping among enemies. He still showed up to work on the food line to feed him, and he still had his job during the day to provide for him, but he was alone, and this was all he knew how to do.

Only now, Tony was different. He felt as though something in him had changed. His patterns were the same, but they were growing old. The seeds that had been planted along the way were starting to grow. He had less desire to continue his patterns, but almost ingrained, he continued. Tony was torn and troubled in his decisions. The life being spoken into him did not line up with the choices he was making.

> "Be alert and of sober mind. Your enemy the devil prowls around like a roaring lion looking for someone to devour" (Peter 5:8).

Night after night, the situation in the apartment escalated, and he just tried to keep himself busy. One night after work, Tony was heading to the apartment earlier than normal looking to get some sleep. Out front, there was a group of men he had often seen from time to time in the apartment. As he approached, he asked one of them for a light for his cigarette, but that request was about to change Tony's life.

The group of men standing there recognized Tony from the apartment. They were taller and bigger than Tony, and he was outnumbered. The men refused his light and started an exchange of words, but soon they were fighting. The thing about having nothing to lose is you are willing to sacrifice anything.

As they fought, the one of the big guys recognized Tony's fearless nature, and it was back and forth for a while. They knocked him down to the ground where Tony struggled to get up. He did not see it coming, but as he stood up to turn around, he saw stars. One of the men in the group had grabbed a chair while he was down. It only took one swing directly to his face, and he was out.

Not sure how long he laid there in that lobby, but soon Tony came to, and the pain in his head was immense, and he could only see out of one eye. The men had scattered at this point, and others just passed by him. Slowly he rose to his feet and stumbled his way back to his own neighborhood looking for protection.

That was a very long night as Tony was in excruciating pain. He could not see out of one eye as his face was so swollen. He was unrecognizable even to himself. Tortured by the pain, he was frustrated that this night he was not looking for the fight, but the fight found him. His only slight protection was just being in his own area, but he was there, and feeling as though he would not make it much longer, he pulled himself together as best he could and made his way to the hospital.

Not wanting to draw trouble, he gave the hospital a fake name. The doctors were obviously concerned about the level of Tony's injuries. They did not push the topic. They helped get him to a stable state knowing only what he told them about getting jumped on the street. As he lay there confused as to why he was still alive, he knew something had to give.

The doctors and the nurses cared for Tony, but they did not know him or where he came from. They did not know the anger and the pain in this man. They were nursing him back to health, but he was nervous they would find out who he was. After four days in the hospital, the swelling had gone down enough for him to see out of both eyes. He was still bruised and swollen, but he was on the mend.

The doctors had made no mention of him being released as he had some significant injuries. Tony though had other thoughts, and after the four days of care, he waited for the doctors to leave. He got up to fetch his clothing from the closet. Once he had dressed himself, he walked out the door to not look back.

Still bruised and swollen, he went back to work to face Frenchy. Frenchy was mad he had missed work, but more than ever, Frenchy the pressure for Tony to get out of the streets got stronger. Frenchy cared for this young man and hated him this way and knowing that there could very well come a day he was gone for good. Frenchy spent that day pouring into him to please change and get out of the streets.

After a fight like that and days in the hospital, he knew the words of Frenchy were correct. He had wanted to change, and after the time spent with Allen in the abandoned building and meeting Diane with the ministry, his heart had been changing.

The words of life were pouring into Tony, and the pull of the enemy was keeping him shackled. Even in his confusion, Tony knew something would have to give way. Either the darkness would devour him or the light would finally break it. Either way, at this point in his life, he was standing at his crossroads.

Tony knew his life was leading to a point of no return. He could hear the words of Frenchy, and he knew that life would need to change. A crossroads in life is often described as the actions you are living no longer matching up with what is in your heart and the two are at conflict. God had been guiding him, but he still felt he could do it on his own. God had been changing Tony's heart to help him see and hear more clearly.

Oftentimes when we find ourselves in bad situations, we are overcome by fear to change the situation. It is often the fear of the unknown. You may have survived for quite some time just hoping for something to change. Maybe what is in need of change is you? Maybe what you need is to stop trying to do this on your own. God did not give us the spirit of fear, the spirit of fear comes from the devil. Put aside your fear and reach out.

CROSSROADS

Thus says the lord: "Stand by the roads, and look, and ask for the ancient paths, where the good way is; and walk in it, and find rest for your souls. But they said, 'We will not walk in it.'

—Jeremiah 6:16, ESV

He had survived the fight, but for how long? He knew who they were, and he had survived, so this would surely cause them to panic. They wanted to finish the job and rid the world of Tony for good. If he returned to the ladies apartment, they would be waiting for him. If he returned to the streets, they would be looking for him.

This was not like the other fights in the past. Before Allen and Diane had come into his life, he would have just went after them all regardless of the consequences, but the last year of his life showed him that there was more. It had him contemplating in a different way and one I am sure he did not expect.

As Frenchy dropped him off and paid him for the day, Tony knew his situation was dire, and he was tired of fighting. He did not go straight for his alcohol and weed. He did not go anywhere. There on the street where he stood was a bench, and feeling anxious and defeated, he sat. He just did not want to continue living this way, he wanted more.

Tony sat there for what seemed like hours lying back, trying to figure out what to do. He knew his trouble was boiling over, and he was stuck and alone. He could not go home, most of his friends had turned away, his brother now gone to start a new life, and he found himself truly stuck and it was time to make a decision.

For so long, Tony had been a man with nothing to lose, a man dangerous to those around him. He lived his anger, and now the last several months, Tony has had life been spoken into him, and he had allowed hope to creep in. The most critical decision of his life was upon him, and the consequences would literally be life or death.

As Tony sat there contemplating what to do next, he put his hands in his pockets. Something was there; he had forgotten he had it. There he pulled out the card from the ministry that Diane had given him when they first met. Holding the card in his hand, he did not jump right away. He sat there for a bit staring at the card, back and forth in his mind if he should even call her.

As Tony stared at the card, he remembered all the prayer and the ministering that Diane had done. His thoughts went to her and her faith. Maybe if Tony called her, he would get some advice and maybe she would know of some resources to help him. Surely if she was truly a woman of God, she would know who could help him. For the first time in his life, he was turning toward God and the people the Lord put in front of him. With no other options, he went to the payphone near his bench and made the phone call.

Imagine how much pride you need to swallow to make that phone call. Here was a man whom was not accustomed to asking for help. He was Ant Rock, and someone as hard as a rock does not need help. Tony had caused this trouble in his three years on the streets and accepting help would have been a humbling experience, but three years of trying to do this on his own was not working, and now he was in more trouble than ever.

It is sometimes the most frustrating thing when we have a problem and no matter what we try to do, it just keeps getting worse. Now Tony was ready to change and do something different in his life, and it meant having to let go of what he was trying to do and rely on another to help.

Tony was desperate for help bigger than he deserved, and he dialed. I can only imagine there was the piece in him that hoped she would not answer when he called, but she did. When she answered, it was a hard discussion as Tony searched for the words to say. Nervous, he did not waste time on formalities, and for the first time in years, he admitted he needed help. He told her about the trouble he was in and how he did not want to die in the streets of Brooklyn. He asked her if he could go to where she was. Without hesitation, she said yes.

A wave of relief came over Tony as he took note of the information to get to where she was. After hanging up the phone, he knew that this was his chance to change. Not sure of what the outcome would be, he gathered himself and headed for the train. Tony did not waste time getting his ticket purchased. He was heading into an unknown situation, and he wanted to get there before the reels started to play in his head.

This was the biggest step Tony had made in his life to this point. As he reflects, he knows the decision he made to go to ask for help was one that saved his life. For so long he had been angry at the world for his situation that his trouble was bound to catch up to him.

He knows now what it is like to hit the rock bottom of life. The feeling of knowing that your next decision would be life or you would accept death. It was almost as if God was telling him that he had provided his path out, but he had to choose darkness or light.

Diane lived just outside the city in Long Island. It took several different connections of trains just to get close to where she was. As he stepped off the train, it was already dark. Diane's ministry was still about a mile away, so in the dark he began to walk. As he arrived, she was there to meet him.

Her ministry building was there and next door was a small house with several rooms. The house was rented to some of the other men who worked in the ministry. He knew it was late, but relieved he had finally arrived.

Having talked to Tony in the lines for food, she had learned of his time on the streets. She knew a little about the trouble he was in and knew how broken he was, but when he arrived, she welcomed Tony like a lost son that had finally come home as they sat down to talk. There was a feeling of being a little overwhelmed by her greeting and how she could so quickly break down the walls he had built up to protect himself.

It was like a flood that comes with a big storm as Tony sat there and just released all the hurt, the pain, the suffering, and all the anger he had carried over the last three years. He did not really hold anything back at this point. As Tony sat there and released his entire world, she gave him her full attention. She listened patiently to the pain he had and never gave judgment. To her, she knew he was tired and worn and finally really ready for his life to change.

Her plan was simple. Tony would come to live in the house next door, he would go to work with Frenchy, and he would come back to work the ministry at night. If he stayed busy, he would not be tempted to go back to the streets. Diane knew healing had to come from God. She could love on him, but the change happens when you let God in. She prayed with him and over him as she helped him to accept God into his life and asking God for forgiveness. Not just for himself, but all the others in his life that had let him down.

It is not an instant change by any means, but there is an instant peace when you just accept God into your life. It had taken three years for God to get Tony's attention, and his acceptance was only the beginning of change. She helped him to speak those words in prayer as he cried and knew that he had chosen light over darkness, and now it was time to heal.

Diane was not one to treat Tony like a child, but a young man that needed guidance. He had only known the streets for the last three years, and these were the years he entered manhood. Without a father around, he was not taught how to be a man or how to really survive. He did not know how to be a man, and she knew it.

She also recognized the influence that Frenchy had in Tony's life. Frenchy was the father figure he needed and provided him a job that would help Tony in his new journey. I am sure she knew the magnitude of the situation with him, but she also knew he was ready to change.

Diane knew when Tony needed soft words, and she knew when he needed tough love. She was a force to be reckoned with. She meant business and managed her food lines with authority, but loved on each person regardless of who they were.

She earned the ultimate respect for her ability to forgive and truly minister to others. Her words meant so much to Tony whether soft or tough, and to this day, she is one woman who can bring him to tears.

The hardest part about change is that it does not happen overnight. You do not accept Jesus and that just suddenly erases twenty-three years of your pain and anguish. Diane knew that, and through it all remained patient with Tony's progress. To him, she seemed so unshakable and one of the strongest individuals he had ever met. Tony followed her light, and change started within him.

After their talk, she walked Tony to the house next door. This would be his new home for now, and to his surprise, while waiting for him, she prepared a room. She informed the other three living there he was coming to stay with them for a while. They knew him from working the line, and they were happy he was there. They would have to split the rent, and four-ways was better than three, so he was welcome to stay.

Tony was overwhelmed with relief and gratitude. Walking into the house with the other three men and how they welcomed him with smiles. It was all a bit overwhelming as he had just fully confessed his life and now had three instant roommates that were happy to see him. It was almost more than Tony could bare, and to this day is full of gratitude to all of them. For the first time in a very long time, he felt wanted.

Like Tony, many of us face crossroads, but this is where change can begin. Once you make the choice to change, the light of God will shine upon you, and you will become new again. Tony did not know how to be an adult, but he had to try. You may not know how you are going to make it through your crossroads, but are you willing to try?

Learning to Live

Therefore, if anyone is in Christ, the new creation has come:[a] The old has gone, the new is here!

—2 Corinthians 5:17, NIV

Tony did not know how to be off the streets and staying busy did help. Every weekday, he would get up early, head to work, come home, work at the ministry, sleep, and repeat.

It was not always easy, and there was one day Tony found himself back in the streets of Brooklyn walking around and reflecting. After all he had been through, those streets looked different. They only held pain of the last three years, and as he felt the emotion welling up inside of him, he quickly left for the train back to Long Island. He was not ready to be back. He walked away and did not look back.

The weekends were no different at the ministry. Tony would spend Friday night preparing to go and feed the homeless the next day. Often working until 11:00 p.m. just to arise and be ready to work by 9:00 a.m. the next morning. There was so much preparation that went into getting ready to feed the homeless. Many times not returning to the ministry home until after 8:00 p.m., they were tired and spent. They would go home to get something to eat, watch a little TV, and not much time later, exhaustion took over, and they would go to bed.

Sundays provided a little more rest. They still had to rise early for church, but after church, Tony took full advantage of his opportunity to catch up on sleep. He was exhausted but in a good way. He was doing good work, he was sober, and he was thinking clearly. God was moving in his life.

Keeping busy was great, but once again Tony learned to rest. He loves his sleep, even today. When given the opportunity, he will take his naps and hates when he misses them. This is something he learned to need and desire as he remembers so vividly how many nights he had to go without.

The day Tony made the phone call, he stopped drinking and doing drugs. It was not easy, and he would often feel like he needed to self-medicate himself, but his desire to change was greater, and he was able to resist. So, for the next several months, he followed his new routine and kept himself out of trouble.

Despite being so busy, Tony found time to read the Bible, and he had learned to pray often. Diane treated him like a human being but kept him accountable to his healing. She welcomed him when he came from work, she asked him about his day, she asked him if he was staying diligent in the word, and many times prayed with him.

The love Tony felt for Diane and how she helped him was like gaining a second mother. She was faithful in her love for him, and it always pushed him to do better. She did not allow him much slack, and he was happy about that. He was learning how to survive outside of the streets and taking what he learned from Frenchy how to be a man.

What if Diane had said no? When you ask Tony this question, a look of bewilderment comes across his face. Then he looks at me and says, "If she had said no, I would be dead right now." There is power in the realization that sometimes our encounters with others could be the difference in someone's life.

It takes a lot to not say no to God when he gives you a big assignment. To be honest, when I first felt the calling to write this, my first reaction was no. The interesting perspective now after all these years was the power this woman had to say no to what God asked of her and seemingly end the life of a man desperate to change, and how no was not even an option for her.

The beautiful thing about living in that house was how well Tony got along with his three other roommates named Hector, Bob, and Pete. They paid their rent and did their work day in and day out. When they were hungry, they were allowed to just go across to the ministry pantry and get whatever food they wanted to eat. It was not a handout as they all had worked so hard for it, but they all did appreciate having the food.

They shared life together, and you had to build some trusts and bonds to make it. As hard as that was for Tony, he found that it was easier because of the environment they were in. The three were in a position of not working, and either had disability or retired. He learned a lot from working side by side with them day in and day out. He often remembers those roommates fondly and how well they made that house worked.

Tony's love for working out came in his time out of the streets. He did not have much equipment, but every day he would build his body stronger. He loved the feeling his muscles had like his heart and mind, and his body reflected how much stronger Tony was becoming. This helped him pass some time, and he found a new way to focus his frustrations. The more he put into his workout, the better he was feeling. He no longer had the desire to go find the next fight to try and relieve his anger.

Tony had survived three years on the streets, and the established order he now had was welcomed and desired. The hard walls of his heart he had built up in the streets were starting to crumble. He was starting to see the glory of God in his life. As each day passed, going back to the streets became less and less important, and his desire to learn and change became the center of his life.

Tony did still carry anger, and he needed to forgive, but with the help of Diane, he prayed every day, and God was easing the anger. After several months of reading the Bible, staying strong in prayer, and living in an environment surrounded by love and acceptance, he fully accepted God in his life.

In Tony's heart, he knew that the only reason he was even still alive was because of God's grace on him. He was finally living his life and not just existing through it. God's light broke the darkness, and every day the light would get bigger. This is when he knew it was time, and he asked Diane to baptize him.

Surrounded by Tony's ministry family, Diane baptized him. His life was now new. It does not mean he was fully healed or he was finished. It meant he was born again from who he was to who he was becoming. From that day forward, there was a bigger place in his heart for God, and he thanked him every day for his survival and the people he put in his life.

Sometimes the funny thing about healing and praying are the tests God will put into your life. Not meant for harm but for growth, we are sometimes tested in our faith. He was content with the life he was living; he was content with the life he left behind. He had been out of the streets for months and had no desire to go back.

His test did come one Saturday afternoon while out feeding the homeless; he turned around to find his mother and one of his sisters standing in front of him.

Facing the Past

> Consider it all joy, my brethren, when you encounter various trials, knowing that the testing of your faith produces endurance. And let endurance have its perfect result, so that you may be perfect and complete, lacking in nothing.
>
> —James 1:2–4

Tony had to do a double take to see if he was really seeing them standing there. Mixed emotions filled him as why would they come now that he was healing, while he was content, and so long after he had been out of the streets? His first instinct would be to turn away as they had done to him, but this was his mother, and he loved her dearly. Instead of pushing them away, Tony embraced his mother.

Tony's mom had been worried and in complete mom fashion scolded him for no one hearing from him or knowing if he was alive or dead. His answer was simple. "I did not want to be found."

That may seem harsh, but the reality was Tony had more peace in those few months working the ministry than he had most of his life. In reality, as much as he loved his mother, Tony would have been content if they never did come to find him. They had not done so when he was in the streets, but he had been praying for the ability to forgive, and his heart did not carry the same anger he once had.

As the shock of them being there wore off and Tony had embraced his mother, he took them over to meet Diane and talked to her about having the afternoon off. It had been over three years since he had seen them, and he needed some answers. Diane knew this was an opportunity for healing so did not hesitate to let him spend some time with his family. She did not control his moves, but he had so much respect for Diane that he was subtly asking her if he was ready for this encounter.

I am not sure we are ever ready for these encounters. The hurt and pain do not just go away, and there is a distinct reality that you cannot handle these alone. God had been teaching Tony about walking with him, and he needed that strength more now than he even realized.

As Tony spoke with his family, his mother had said she had not known that he had been homeless. It was not until she had come to visit that she had heard the truth. No one had seen or heard from him in months, so quickly her panic set in and for quite some time, they had been calling hospitals, jails, and morgues trying to find him. It was not until several days earlier they had talked to his brother Allen that they heard he was off the streets living and working with the ministry.

I can only imagine what was going through their minds to stand there watching Tony cleaned up, strong, sober, and serving others. Would there be guilt, shame, pride, or joy? The man standing before them was not the same boy they had known. It was a risk for them to seek him out, but his mother had a strong desire to know her boy was okay.

As they headed to the city together, his mom asked Tony to come and live with her in Pennsylvania. She would give him a home and food, and he could be with her. He was touched and almost torn, but he declined her offer.

He had his job with Frenchy and a father figure that he had never had. He had Diane who was teaching him how to survive outside the streets. He had God and an environment that was safe for him, so despite his love for his mother, Tony knew he had to press forward where he was.

Being a mother myself, I am sure that when Tony declined the offer, there was a pain she felt. This was her child, and she wanted him in her life, but as a mother, we also know that at some point you do not mess with a good thing.

Diane and Frenchy were good influences in his life, and he was stronger than ever being in that environment. Her love for Tony's wellbeing gave her understanding, and she did not push the issue.

Now I am sure that most would find this hard to believe. Saying it out loud does seem so unlikely that she did not know for three years that Tony was in the streets alone. As he pressed into this part of the story, it did seem so unbelievable, but he did not question it or push the situation as this was Tony's heart, his mother, and she showed up. While the truth of that will never be fully told, Tony forgave his mother the moment he turned and saw her standing there.

Returning to the city for the first time since the day Tony wandered into the projects came with mixed emotions. There was hesitancy about the lure of the streets, and the hesitancy that his anger might return in a flash. Tony knew he needed to go and face this, but he did not want to go backwards.

Here, Tony sat in the apartment that he was locked out of over three years ago. He could feel the emotion building inside him, and it was hard to contain. It was no mistaking that the pain and anger were still present. He had made progress because the rage was gone, but to be back in that environment and that apartment was a raw pain he was not sure fully how to face.

Tony kept most of his emotion bottled up for that visit and did spend time with his family. After a while, Tony hit a point when he knew it was time to leave and head back to the ministry. He said goodbye to his mother and headed out the door.

Tony had made it through this first step of returning to the apartment since the day he was locked out. He had not lost his temper, and he had no major outbursts. The visit was good for his time with his mother. His forgiveness for his mother was easier, but he did not really want much to do with his sisters, and it was going to take a little more time to reach forgiveness for them.

> Get rid of all bitterness, rage and anger, brawling and slander, along with every form of malice.

> Be kind and compassionate to one another, forgiving each other, just as in Christ God forgave you. (Ephesians 4:31–32)

A few visits later, Tony knew he had some unfinished business. He had not been back to the ladies apartment since the night of the fight. He knew there were just a few things still there he wanted to retrieve. Knowing the possibility of running into the men that put him in the hospital, he took two of his brothers with him to have his back.

The lady in the apartment was so happy to see him. She had always suspected he had been in jail or worse. She knew about the fight in the lobby and was just grateful he was standing there alive. The men were not there, so he talked with her for a few minutes, gathered his remaining items, and left.

Part of facing Tony's past was not just forgiveness for his family. It was forgiveness for himself and his actions. You do not spend three years on the streets just because your sisters locked you out. You do not spend three years on the streets just because your father left when you were five. You spend three years on the streets because your choices in life started long before you were locked out. You spend three years in the streets because you let the streets and all the false promises consume you with darkness.

Before Tony could forgive the others, he had to forgive himself. This would be the harder task of acceptance, responsibility for his part, and to heal those parts of him that were broken. He had made it this far, and he was determined to keep going.

I am sure if you talked with them all today, his sisters were pretty tired of Tony's constant questions about why they put him out and not being satisfied with their answers. Over the years, the answers became less important than forgiveness. He loves his sisters, and having developed a bit of a relationship with them over the years, he knows they are all further from who they were at that time.

Tony's love for them did not go away, and he will call them from time to time today and talk. He has had to learn ways of having relationships with them and not because he holds hate, but because of how his life has been changed. They had their own experiences of hurt and pain that have impacted their lives, and they were contributors to his experience, but not the overall cause.

The Bible consistently talks about forgiveness. Sometimes the pain and hurt can be so overwhelming that forgiveness is not easy to come by. The thing that Tony has learned about forgiveness over the years is how forgiveness does not take away the responsibility for other people's actions, but is allowing you to not be controlled by the pain others have caused. It does not mean relationship, but it does mean real freedom.

When you look back over your life, think of the people who need forgiveness?

New Life

> The righteous keep moving forward, and those with clean hands become stronger and stronger.
>
> —Job 17:9

During Tony's time in the ministry church was an important part of his new life. It was at church he had met a woman named Liza. After some time, they started dating. She worked at the ministry with him, and they were growing closer. This was his first real relationship, and it was nice to have her working in the same ministry and going to the same church. They connected and had a lot of fun with each other.

Living in a tight routine of staying busy constantly, Tony was able to save money even with dating. Dating was just another element to try and balance. So, in order for Liza to get close to him, she had to fit into his schedule, which meant most dates were working in the ministry. Romantic, right? Well, it was what Tony could give, and she seemed content to date a man that kept himself busy serving others.

After a while, the ministry moved locations in Long Island to another building. The men stayed in the house, and they traveled back and forth to the new location. Hector had been seeing a woman from the ministry, and they were talking marriage. Right around the same time, Bob just disappeared. With Hector wanting to get married and Bob gone, it was clear that Tony and Pete would not be able to afford the rent of that house between the two of them.

The owner was okay with the thought of them moving as he was ready to sell the home. Pete was pretty resourceful and quickly found them each a room upstairs from this Italian family. It was like two small one-room apartments that they could have on their own.

It was an outside entrance on top of an older house. This move would be perfect for them, and it was closer to where the ministry had moved. Tony and Pete would continue to be neighbors, and they prepared to move.

On the day they moved, Tony took a huge step in his learning to trust. He had been keeping his money saved up under his pillow, but on the day of the move, Tony had to work with Frenchy, and he did not want to carry the money to work. He approached Pete and asked him to hold the money he was hiding under his pillow until he returned from work.

Pete's eyes grew and immediately asked Tony where he got so much money. Tony laughed as he explained that he had been saving it up since getting off the streets. He knew it was a lot to ask Pete, but they had grown close, and he felt he could trust him with his money.

Now this was still Ant Rock, and Pete understood that. This made Pete a little uncomfortable with that much money. So to keep him from losing Tony's money, Pete took the money to Diane. That day, Pete earned Tony's trust, and Diane knew she needed to help him get an account for that money.

When they arrived at the new place, Tony was excited. The room was not much more than a small room. No bigger than a regular-sized living room, but he did not care. It was his, and this is a point when he knew he was making it.

Now that he was out of the streets and getting stronger, Frenchy began to push Tony to get his license so he could learn to drive the truck. Only having just a few lessons from his father in North Carolina, his girlfriend Liza helped him learn to drive, and he got his license.

At the same time Tony was learning to drive, Frenchy started showing him how to drive the big trucks. He had the books, studied, and where else would you learn to drive a CDL truck but the streets of Manhattan. It was hard at times, and Frenchy did a lot of yelling, but Tony finally got it down and passed his test for a CDL.

He had managed to get a car to help him get around faster. It was an old Citation that was beat-up and tattered. Tony really liked that car, but most likely because the car, like him, had been through a lot and just kept on running.

Tony remembers one day driving through Brooklyn heading back to his home in Long Island. There on the street was one of the men from the fight he had. The man was haggard, and the streets had taken a toll on him. There was a moment when the urge came up to run him over for what they did to him, but that was not what God was asking him to do. So, instead, he made peace in that moment and continued on his way.

It was after some time that Tony's relationship with Liza grew into the direction of marriage. She had been having trouble where she was living, and through a series of events, she moved in with him. This was difficult on many levels because it was just a small one-room apartment meant for one person. Now with two, they were cramped. More than being cramped, it meant disappointing Diane, and needless to say, she was less than thrilled about the arrangement.

Tony's time with the ministry ended shortly after that as him and Liza set out to get a bigger apartment together. It was not negative separation from the ministry, and he is not lost on all it had done for him. He was still newer to his faith, but for the first time in his life, he felt he was ready to move on.

This opened up Tony's ability to spend weekends going back and forth to visit his mother. He would take time and ensure she was taken care of, take her shopping, and just overall rebuilding a relationship with her.

It was so important to Tony that he had the ability to help her in her retirement and even at times helping some of his nephews nearby get shoes for their feet. He was now taking care of his own in ways his mom had in his youth. His growth had made him keenly aware that it is always important to help others even if they cannot do anything for you in return.

Over the years, this mentality grew and expanded beyond family. It is something he feels very strongly about today. How helping others that have nothing to give you in return are privileges given to us all.

Frenchy wanted Tony to take over the route and eventually buy it from him as Frenchy was working toward retiring. Oh how Tony thought about doing that, but the truth is, he knew that he needed out of the city before the streets called him home. His need to be away from the streets kept him from buying that route.

Years later talking to Frenchy, you knew he was so happy for Tony and to see how far he had come. Frenchy had always wished he would buy the route, but he understood why Tony could not. To this day, he has never had a boss like Frenchy. The impact Frenchy had on him would surpass further than I know he ever expected.

That CDL was a ticket for Tony. It meant a better life, normal money, and he could go anywhere and use this ticket. His possibilities were endless, and he explored so many throughout the years.

The hard part about raising children is in knowing when you have completed your task and they must now take up their life and make it into something more. This was what we had to face when we moved and our daughter stayed behind. There were many tears shed, but an understanding that this was the right thing to do.

Are you holding onto something you do not want to let go of? What if your blessings come when you let go?

Life Moves On

Brothers, I do not consider that I have made it my own. But one thing I do: forgetting what lies behind and straining forward to what lies ahead.

—Philippians 3:13

Tony was twenty-seven years old, and he had made it out of the city altogether. Knowing the pull the streets have on people, he made a decision to marry Liza and move to South Dakota. Now that is a far cry from any city he ever has known, but the streets were further away, and he could continue to grow.

Just before the marriage and leaving for South Dakota, Tony was in the projects visiting family. He was on his way home that afternoon when he ran into Roger. This was the first time Tony had seen Roger since their fallout years before. Like old friends, the happiness to see each other outweighed the issues they had years before. This particular meeting would bring reconciliation that has meant the world to Tony for years.

As they stood there talking, Roger openly talked to Tony about how he hated seeing his friend self-destruct. Watching Tony spiral hurt him, and the only thing he knew was to push him away. Knowing the life Tony was living and the anger he carried, he knew his friend was right.

They talked for a moment and wished each other well, not knowing that this would be the last time Tony would see that friend. Oh how grateful he is to this day just to know he was able to see Roger this one last time.

After his marriage, Tony took the first steps to leave New York and move to South Dakota. It was a culture shock and very different world from the streets Tony knew. He knew South Dakota would not be his permanent home, but it was out of the street.

After a while, he was missing his mother and needed to visit home. Tony's mom was going to the apartment in Brooklyn to visit, so with a few days off, he packed the car and alone took the thirty-hour trip by car to see his family.

While there, Tony ran into some friends he had known growing up. They were on the street hanging out, and he was so happy to see them. Tony invited them into his car to hang out for a while and catch up. Here were two men who had last seen Tony homeless in the street with no hope. They had just figured he was a victim of the street until the man standing before them showed up.

In shock, they started with the questions. What happened to him? Had Tony really done that drive alone? How could this person be sitting with them have ever gotten out of that situation he was in? Tony began to tell them about his experience and how God saved his life. Tony was who he was only because of God.

Both men listened intently as they sat in amazement. Does God really save the broken? The truth Tony was telling them is no matter how far you fall, you can always be saved. It was easy to tell them this story because they knew him when he was lost. After a while, they said their goodbyes, and Tony returned home to South Dakota.

It wasn't until years ago that Tony connected with one of the men in the car that day that he heard about his impact. His friend was living in another state with a wife and two kids and had a good life outside of the streets. His friend began sharing with Tony how his story touched him, and after Tony left, he knew he needed to change. Now he was living a life he did not think he could have because he knew that God would save him too.

Tony was humbled by this story and grateful that his experience could have had such impact on another person's life. This friend saw him at his worst and could see how he was saved.

The further Tony got from the streets and the more people he met in life, Tony found it easier to not share this testimony in his life. Forgiveness helped him heal from the anger and rage, but the pain of that time still lingered. These people he was meeting now knew him as the man he was, so leaving that old person behind became easier.

Life is about choices. The ebb and flow of life where you will fall, you will rise, you will overcome. Far away from the streets, Tony's marriage to Liza was ending. They were young and not ready for the relationship they were trying to have. Through another series of events, he left South Dakota and wound up in Colorado.

Colorado was not his first choice by any means, but God has a way of putting you where he needs you. Tony would spend the next eighteen years of his life in Colorado living a life he never dreamed was possible when he was twenty. This is where he built the life he has today.

It is said you see God's work in reverse. God is guiding you while he goes before you. Often you do not see the true miracle until later. So many times Tony should have died; the fights he had or the nights on the bridge, yet every morning when the dawn broke the night, he was alive, and now he was living a completely different life with a family of his own. Some would probably argue these facts, but that was supernatural.

Tony did not go from rags to riches like you see in the movies, but he did come from the bottom and has worked tirelessly to make a life for himself. He uses that CDL Frenchy helped him get even today and keeps faith front and center in the relationships he builds today.

Tony's life is a far cry from where he came from. His life is about healing, and Tony's life is about forgiveness. When learning to walk, you will take some falls, but the getting up is the glorious part. Three years in the streets taught him about staying down, and the two years with the ministry taught him about rising.

The reconciliations of his past have helped Tony become the father he is today. It has helped him become the friend he is today. His reconciliations have taught him about not giving up when life gets hard. People in his life have come and gone. All of which helped him in some way to grow.

I would like to say I am the love of his life, but the truth is, I will always be number 2 behind Tony's relationship with God. That is how it should be and an expectation I have in our life. It allows us to flow in ways that keep us fully connected. Yes, even when we are on each other's nerves to the point of frustration.

Life delivered some blows in his family. Sitting in reflection on these times, Tony has found blessings in knowing he was not only able to forgive but have some relationships with them before it was too late.

After getting out of the streets, he learned his father had come back to New York. He connected with his father, and they were able to have a small relationship together. His father came to his first wedding, and even though he would move across the country, they would call each other from time to time.

On the day Tony's father called and said he was going to the hospital to die, he was not sure if his father was serious. It was such a final statement and so completely out of the blue. This is when his father told him about his cancer, and he had now reached a point in his life where he knew it was the end. His father did not want to call until he was essentially checking himself into the hospital hospice area. Without hesitation, Tony packed a bag and went to him.

Tony felt truly blessed that he was there with his father in the last week of his life. Talking to him, praying for him, and showing him love. The little boy kept expecting him to get up and say it was all a joke, but seeing him in that bed in and out of consciousness, he knew the truth.

It was two days before Christmas, and they had all been preparing to go to the hospital when the call came that his father had passed away. For his father, it was probably important to die when they were not present, but there was peace in knowing they all came.

His father was broken like everyone else. He did not understand how to be a father, but he was Tony's father and despite his faults, he was deserving of love.

Several years later, Tony's mother's health had started to fall. She had several strokes, and each one bound her to the bed even more. We were blessed that during this time his mother did come to stay with us for a short period of time. It was out of love that he wanted to help her and out of love when his oldest sister came to take her back home to New York.

Tony's mom always had a way of calling at crazy times. Sometimes she would call at 2:00 a.m., sometimes at midnight; it never seemed to matter. You take for granted those times because it breaks your sleep, but on the day Tony was home working on the floors of the house, the call came that she had passed away.

A piece of Tony's heart left with her that day. His love for his mother was so deep, and the thought of her being gone devastated him. Being several states away, we packed up and took the forty-five-hour drive. In his emotion, he did not stop to sleep. We would take turns driving, and he will not say record time, but he needed to get to New York to be with his family.

Her struggle was over, and although Tony wanted her back, he knew her place in heaven would be magnificent. He knew he was blessed to have this woman in his life. She is the one that instilled in him the seeds of life he still carries today.

Over the years, most of Tony's family have all scattered out of the streets of New York. Only one sister even remains in the city teaching and going to church in her community while his youngest sister lives in a group home nearby. Their lives are all different and shaped in some way by the streets they called home.

Frenchy retired a few years after Tony left New York. He found another driver to take over the route and did eventually sell it to him. When in New York, we do always cross the bridge to go and see Frenchy and his family. They still talk so openly and freely as if it was just yesterday they saw each other.

Frenchy is humble and does not take much credit for the impact he had in Tony's life. There is a love for this man that showed him a fatherly love that Tony so desperately needed. How he never gave up on a young man in the pit of his despair.

Diane still works her ministry. Sadly, years ago, someone came in the night and burned the ministry building to the ground. There is rumor it was one of Tony's old roommates that came to destroy. Whoever it was, they were desperate and angry and was taking it out on the ministry that was helping others. The thing about living to serve God, you can bend it, but you will never break it. With a rally of help, they rebuilt stronger than before.

As they can and thanks to social media, they have been able to reconnect. There is not much Tony's spiritual mother can say that will not bring him back to perspective. She always knows the words to say to him to keep him grounded.

He may never know, but knowing what she did in his life, he can only imagine just how many others have found salvation because of her. This woman is truly a gift from God, and his love for her will never die.

Sowing and Reaping

> Very truly I tell you, unless a kernel of wheat falls to the ground and dies, it remains only a single seed. But if it dies, it produces many seeds.
>
> —John 12:24

One big truth that is laced in Tony's life today is in the seeds that were being sown and what was reaped. As a child, his mother sowed into him the seeds of work ethic, and his brother sowed into him the desire to stay out of jail, and God used those seeds at just the right moment in his life when he needed them.

Tony's decision at eighteen to stop selling drugs and get a regular job may have seemed like something pretty insignificant, but the truth is, this decision was the moment those seeds were reaped, and God was able to put a light in his life for the darker days to come. His protection was set in motion by God before his other decisions would put him on the streets.

His decision to not jump when he found himself on the rooftop or bridge allowed God to open the door for his brother to find him. Reaping the seeds of family, he allowed himself to forgive his brother and go stay with him. This all led to his introduction to Diane.

The seeds of hope that Diane had been sowing into him while he worked in the lines for food broke down many walls. God used these seeds so in the most crucial point of his life, the seeds of hope allowed him to ask for help.

Tony lives by the principle that the choices you make today will show their impact in the future. There is always a desire to keep doing things on your own when your flesh feels God is taking too long. This is when trials will arrive, but with each trial, God shows up, and you become stronger in your faith than you were before.

Tony's life is now consumed with breaking patterns.

"He led them from the darkness and deepest gloom; he snapped their chains" (Psalms 107:14).

In his life, God worked such miracles. God kept Tony alive when he so easily could have died. God kept him from getting sick living in those streets every day. In all of Tony's anger and all his pain, God kept a light in his path, never letting it go completely out. Tony fought the light for so long, but God stayed, and as the shields of invincibility started crumbling around him, God used those as opportunities to add more light until he was ready to be saved.

Today you will often find Tony wearing something with a NY symbol on it. It is a reminder of the streets he survived and where he found his savior.

On the radio, you hear so many raps and songs about life in the streets. You see movies that sometimes get close, but there is no glamour in the life Tony came from. The logos he wears are more about survival than they are about pride of where he came from. From time to time, Tony will run into someone that came from the projects like him. Their paths had never crossed until that moment, and yet there is an instant understanding they have when they talk.

Tony always knows the ones that claim to be from the streets because unless you have lived it, you may not fully understand the pull they have on a person's life. The real ones know by the symbol of the streets that this person survived and there is almost an instant connection in the few moments they talk.

Now nestled in Arizona, Tony's journey is not close to complete, and he knows that more will come. Praying every day, he continues to be blessed by God. His life since the streets has not been perfect or free of sin. He has still weathered storms and had to grow from choices, but each day God renews him.

Tony still connects as much as possible with others from that time. Not to drudge up the past but to remember who he is and where he has come from. His heart is full of joy and love for those that loved him when he was unlovable.

This process has already allowed perspective in Tony's life. The value of what he is sowing into the kids, and the value of what was sowed into him. With each step, God had perfect timing. We may all be impatient at times with the timing of God and you may not know what tomorrow brings, but God knows.

If you are out there and trying to do this alone, just know that God is there and working. With each night that comes, there is always a dawn that will come and break the night. Let God shine the light in your life and show you just how loved you are.

About the Author

Melissa Aytche has been in corporate leadership for over fifteen years leading teams of people to success in their careers. Her study of leadership and human emotion is now taken to another level by bridging the gap between human emotion and the Bible. Taking on very personal stories to bring perspective to our lives today and how they intertwine with God's grace.